# LOST TREASURES
# OF THE
# MEDITERRANEAN WORLD

BY ROBERT PAYNE

*The Gold of Troy*
*The Splendor of Greece*
*Journey to Persia*
*The White Pony*
*Forever China*
*The Shepherd*
*The Three Worlds of Albert Schweitzer*

# LOST TREASURES OF THE MEDITERRANEAN WORLD

*Robert Payne*

THOMAS NELSON & SONS

*Edinburgh* NEW YORK *Toronto*

 Published in New York by Thomas Nelson & Sons and simultaneously in Toronto, Canada, by Thomas Nelson & Sons (Canada) Limited.

*Library of Congress Catalog Card Number: 62–16354*

DESIGN BY FRANK KARPELES

*Manufactured in the United States of America*

FOR TRUX AND LUCY

*and the treasure they will find*

# ACKNOWLEDGEMENTS

Many people have been helpful in the preparation of this book, and I am especially grateful to Dr. Rodney S. Young of the University of Pennsylvania Museum, Philadelphia; Miss Lucy Shoe of the American School of Classical Studies, Princeton; Dr. Stuart M. Shaw of the Metropolitan Muesum, New York; Dr. Paul Underwood of the Byzantine Institute, Dumbarton Oaks; and Mr. Edward Ochsenschlager of the Department of Classics, New York University.

Grateful acknowledgement for permission to reproduce photographs is made to: Agora Excavations, American School of Classical Studies, Athens, for pictures on pages 90, 92, 96, 97, 99, 100; Alinari for pictures on pages 83, 87, 89 (upper and lower); American Friends of the Hebrew University, New York, for pictures on pages 203 (upper and lower), 210, 211; American School of Classical Studies, Athens, for pictures on pages 129, 130 (upper and lower), 131, 132 (upper and lower); Anatolian Research Project of the Department of Classics, New York University, for pictures on pages 170, 171, 172, 173, 174; Archaeological Research Fund, New York University, for pictures on pages 134, 135; Archives Photographiques, Paris, for pictures on pages 31, 35, 36, 39, 40, 43, 44; Archivio Fotografico, Musei Vaticani, Rome, for pictures on pages 64, 67 (upper and lower), 68, 70; Alexander Artemakis for picture on page 17; Assessorato Turismo—Spettacolo della Regione Siciliana, Palermo, for pictures on pages 85, 86; Carlo Bavagnoli for picture on page 106; Professor G. E. Bean, Constantinople, for picture on page 168; British Broadcasting Corporation, Photographic Service, for picture on page 33 (lower); British Museum for picture on page 103; Byzantine Institute, Dumbarton Oaks, for pictures on pages 150, 152–53, 156, 159, 161, 163; Chambon, Châtillon-sur-Seine, for picture on page 34; Deutsches Archäologisches Institut, Athens, for pictures on pages 136, 139 (left and right), 141 (upper and lower); Édition du Temps, Paris, for pictures from *Glanum* by Henri Rolland on pages 46, 49 (lower), 51, 52 (upper and lower), 53; European Picture Service, New York, for picture on page 202; Fondazione Ing. C. M. Lerici and Superintendant of Antiquities of Southern Etruria for pictures on pages 62, 63; French Embassy Press & Information Division, New York, for pictures on pages 38, 49 (upper); Gabinetto Fotografico Nazionale, Rome, for picture on page 88; Robert Emmett Ginna for pictures on pages 54, 58; Theresa Goell for pictures on pages 184, 186, 187, 188, 191; Theresa Goell and Dr. F. K. Doerner for picture on page 190; Government of Israel Press Office, Tel Aviv, for pictures on pages 192, 196, 200 (upper and lower), 205, 206; Hirmer Verlag, Munich, for pictures on pages 71, 72, 73, 74, 146, 147, 148; Dr. J. J. Hutt, Strasbourg, for picture on page 33 (upper); Israel Government Tourist Corporation, Tel Aviv, for picture on page 204; Israel Office of Information, New York, for pictures on pages 194, 209; Italian Government Tourist Office, New York, for picture on page 80; David Lees for pictures on pages 56, 60; Spyros Meletzes for pictures on pages 19, 21; Royal Greek Embassy Information Service, New York, for pictures on pages 22, 95, 98, 102, 104, 108, 109, 110, 112, 113, 115 (upper and lower), 116, 117, 118, 120, 122, 123, 124, 126; Dr. Stuart M. Shaw, Metropolitan Museum, New York, for pictures on pages 213, 215 (upper and lower), 216, 217 (upper and lower); Soprintendenza alle Antichita, Salerno, for pictures on pages 76, 77, 79; United Nations, New York, for picture on page 218; Dr. Rodney S. Young, University of Pennsylvania Museum, Philadelphia, for pictures on pages 176, 178, 181, 183 (upper and lower); Yugoslav Information Center, New York, for pictures on pages 142, 143, 145.

CONTENTS

ILLUSTRATIONS

# INTRODUCTION

IN THE beginning there was a Golden Age. So we learn from the ancients, but it is only recently that we have come to believe them. Nearly three thousand years ago Hesiod gave noble expression to the belief that there was a time "when men lived like gods, with calm untroubled minds, free from all toil and anguish." The Golden Age perished as a result of human perversity, and was followed by a Silver and a Bronze Age, and these in turn were followed by the sinister Iron Age in which Hesiod himself lived. The same legend was related by Ovid, who regaled his countrymen with stories of a miraculous and peaceful age before the march of the legionaries had converted the world into an armed camp. Meanwhile, beyond the eastern shores of the Mediterranean, the Hebrews had been perfecting their visionary legends of the Garden of Eden. In nearly all mythologies we find these legends of a happy and blessed state at the dawn of time.

For the past eighty or ninety years archaeologists have been showing us that there is some substance in these dreams. In Crete and in Egypt and on the Greek mainland they have uncovered civilizations where the people seem to have been less troubled than ourselves, and where the arts of life were cultivated with a quiet charm and a deep earnestness derived from their worship of the gods, which gave meaning to their lives. The archaeologists have uncovered many Golden Ages.

As they go about the task of uncovering one buried city after another, the archaeologists find themselves inescapably involved in a strange dialogue. The past speaks to them with a seductive voice. They find the letters of lovers buried in the sands, inscriptions carved on mountains and on cooking vessels, and the stray gossip of the market place is inscribed on walls. More trustworthy even than the written word are the habits and customs of peoples as recorded in their jewelry, their furniture, the carvings and sculptures in which they have depicted for posterity their way of life. To the patient archaeologist the past is vividly alive. He comes to know the faces and the intimate habits of people who died so long ago that he can only guess when they lived. Sometimes he will come to know them almost as well as he knows his friends. Time vanishes. The past comes into its own.

When time vanishes, when all the intervening seasons and years dissolve into nothingness like a pricked balloon, then a number of quite extraordinary things happen. Your archaeologist, trained to logical habits of thought, finds logic small help to him. He had best think of these people in purely human terms, or not at all. He must discard, too, all his luggage of theories about the orderly upward progress of civilization and the social improvement and perfectibility of man on earth, for he will discover that progress is neither orderly nor upward, and social improvement is a nearly meaningless term. He will discover that many of the laws of nature are held in abeyance, and that it is in his power to bring about the resurrection of the dead. Among other things, he will discover that the dead can be extremely vocal, and sometimes they will ask troubling questions.

In the continuing dialogue which the archaeologist holds with the past, all the best lines come from the dead. More often than he would like, the archaeologist finds himself acting the role of the cub reporter interviewing venerable old men of towering genius. Gudea, Moses, Sennacherib, Minos, Pericles pass in review. If we do not hear their authentic voices, at least we hear voices not unlike those discovered by Michael Ventris when he deciphered an ancient Cretan script and discovered it to be "a muffled form of Greek, as spoken by a countryman with a mouth full of stones." And with the heroes of the past come the vast processions of the common people, and these too we are beginning to know as we never knew them before. The earth is crowded with their bones, and we have a right to know them.

One of the first lessons learned by the archaeologist is that the past is continually being born. He scrapes the earth carefully, counting the layers as foresters count the rings of trees, and it amuses him to give dates to each separate layer, defending the dates with a welter of scholarly footnotes; but in his heart he knows that it is all preposterous. Art does not move by years. It moves by great spiritual strides in the timeless wandering of peoples. The great artist lives and suffers and dies within a small time-span, but great art is like the eternal sun, which has no noon nor evening nor any night. The great works of art stand together, and we place a statue of Gudea beside the great Poseidon found off Cape Artemision with no feeling that they were produced in different epochs. They are the works of men who have slipped out of time altogether.

The archaeologist in his mysterious traffic with the past is continually being astonished by the modernity of the ancients. He shows surprise when he discovers that the drainage at Knossos in 1450 B.C. is superior to the drainage in his own house, and that the faces of the Knossans are very like the faces of the people he knows; and when he goes further afield and studies the faces of the ancient Egyptians in 3000 B.C., he has a further shock in store for him, for he discovers that they, too, resemble the men he meets every day in the streets. Then he discovers that the arts of the Egyptians and the Knossans are superior to his own, and he learns humility in the face of the prodigious achievements of the past. A man digging among ancient graves can have all his pride knocked out of him.

We have no buildings so beautiful as the temples built by the ancient Greeks. Our furniture is inferior to the furniture of Periclean Athens, and our jewelry is so far inferior to the jewelry found in Egypt and Sumeria that we may well give up making it. Our laws are no great improvement on the laws of the Medes and Persians, and our methods of warfare are not conspicuously preferable to the methods of the ancients. We have electric light, but the glow of an oil lamp gives a warmer texture to human features. We travel faster, and will soon be traveling right off the earth; but we have almost lost the sense of place, a man's reverence for the earth he lives on. To the archaeologist few things are clearer than the abiding love of the ancients for the earth.

But while the archaeologist remains the dedicated servant of the past, it would be a mistake to assume that he is entirely passive. His power increases with every discovery he makes. He has only to dig a small hole in the earth and all our textbooks have to be revised. Schliemann dug up a shaft grave ten feet broad and ten feet long, with the result that five hundred years were added to the history of Greece. Evans dug up a small palace in Knossos and added a thousand years to the history of Crete. These are not isolated examples. The archaeologists are continually invading prehistory, and there is no knowing when the process will stop.

In our grandchildren's time we may expect history books of Europe to begin confidently around 4000 B.C.

In our own age the archaeologist occupies a place of special importance. It is not only that he is perpetually reminding us of a vanished Golden Age, and wielding his magic wand to bring the dead to life, but there is a sense in which he is the intermediary between the past and the present, the vehicle through which the past can speak to us. The past is as essential to us as light and air, for we are rootless without it, and by uncovering the past the archaeologist brings us into our inheritance. He carries on his shoulders the weight of history. Without him we would not know who we are.

## II

We speak of archaeology being a science, and so perhaps it is, but it is more often an art. The archaeologist as artist is no new phenomenon. Schliemann, dedicated to the Homeric heroes and seeing life through the eyes of Homer, came to an abandoned hill in Asia Minor and announced that he had discovered ancient Troy. He went on to unearth gold diadems, and announced that he had discovered the regalia of the Trojan kings; and later at Mycenae he spoke of finding the body of Agamemnon. Some sixth sense told him where to look, but what he found was not what he sought. We are not sure even now whether the hill was Troy, and we are quite certain that the barbaric gold diadems were never worn by Helen. Horace Walpole invented the word "serendipity" to describe the accidental discovery of great things by people searching for something else. Serendipity would seem to be the most valuable article in an archaeologist's luggage.

We speak of archaeologists having a flair for the past, a deep and comprehensive knowledge of that small area beneath the earth's surface where the past is buried, but it is not always, or even very often, that the trained archaeologist brings to light the greatest treasure. The trained archaeologist is at the mercy of his training and his sense of logical order. He knows where to look and where to dig, but sometimes he forgets that for most people life has always been illogical and disorderly, and that the most precious objects of all are disposed of in the most childish ways. Very often the best archaeologists are those who have a faculty for the wildest imaginable guesswork.

The history of archaeology is largely a series of accidents. The greatest

The Poseidon of Artemision

treasures, the really staggering objects, have a habit of falling into our laps. A peasant wandering across a field at night kicks a stone and sees the gleam of buried gold. A farmer, digging a sewage trench, may come upon a hoard of silver cups. This happened recently in England. Not long ago another farmer in a small village near Dijon was ruminating about the presence of some scattered stones in a cabbage field; he dug below the stones and found a hoard of treasure which could only have come from ancient Greece at the time of its greatest splendor. No one knows what it was doing in that French cabbage field. For all we know, Greek treasures may still turn up in England and Scandinavia. The two accomplices of the archaeologist are always the improbable and the accidental.

Consider, for example, the discovery which many believe to be the greatest single treasure recovered in our time from ancient Greece. It happened that in 1926 some sponge fishermen diving off Cape Artemision, the northern tip of the island of Euboea, brought up the left arm of a great bronze statue. The arm was nearly three feet long, undamaged, with every finger in place. It was taken to the laboratories of the National Museum, examined, and placed in a bath of distilled water. It seemed unlikely that anything more would be heard about it.

Two years later Dr. Alexander Benakis, the possessor of a renowned museum of the arts in Athens, decided to present some diving equipment to the Greek government for underwater excavations. Someone remembered the long bronze arm lying in the National Museum, and suggested that divers be sent down into the dangerous waters off Cape Artemision. There was a faint—a very faint—hope that the rest of the figure might be found. With an escort from the Greek navy, the divers dropped twenty fathoms at a point some 600 yards from the northern tip of Euboea, and almost immediately they came upon the rest of the statue, a magnificent naked god, nearly seven feet tall. Two other bronzes, a boy rider and the forepart of a rearing horse, were also found, together with some bronze ribbons which may have formed part of the composition of the boy on horseback. The strong current had swept the horse and boy away from the ancient shipwreck. What else was on the sunken ship no one knows, for the search was abandoned when one of the divers, refusing to use the foreign equipment given by Dr. Benakis, dived deep and then rapidly surfaced. Emerging from the water, he laughed at his less venturesome colleagues, and dropped dead from ruptured blood vessels.

The Poseidon of Artemision

The bronze god was encrusted with marine growths and lacked a small fragment of the right calf, but was otherwise miraculously unharmed. To remove the marine growths and to preserve the rich reddish patina, the statue was placed in a bath of distilled water; nothing else was allowed to touch it. For two years the experts in the National Museum watched over the statue and planned how the once-missing arm should be joined to it. Finally it was put on display.

This bronze Poseidon, found piecemeal and over an interval of years, is the supreme achievement of Greek sculpture, the most powerful and majestic representation of a Greek god known to us. He stands poised with an invisible trident in his right hand, the left arm extended and pointing along the weapon's course, which he follows with his eyes, once set with jewels, now dark and cavernous. His hair and beard fall in heavy curls, according to the style prevalent at the end of the sixth century B.C. His powerful body is balanced on the left foot, and he barely touches the ground with the right. Every muscle is in tension, but he gives an overwhelming impression of calm. The face is of a divine eminence, ruthless and gentle, possessing a majesty almost beyond comprehension. Never before or afterwards, as far as we know, did the Greeks make a statue of such awesome grandeur and superhuman power.

Compared with this Poseidon, "the lord of the flaming trident," the famous Charioteer of Delphi is no more than a dreaming boy. We know now why the Greeks felt such awe before the great Zeus by Phidias at Olympia, though that statue was draped in patterned gold sheeting, and this is superbly naked. Athena, looking down from her throne in the Parthenon, must have had the same majesty, but she too was clothed and so richly ornamented that she seemed to hide behind her veils. Poseidon reveals himself completely.

We can only guess who the artist was and when the statue was made. We know that in 480 B.C. the Persian fleet was destroyed in a great storm in the bay between the island of Euboea and Thermopylae, and for raising this storm the Greeks in gratitude, as we learn from Herodotus, gave Poseidon the title of Savior, "which they used ever afterward when speaking his name." Clearly the statue represents Poseidon the Savior, the divine protector and avenger of injuries, at the very moment when the injury is avenged and divine protection is being offered to the Greeks. By that storm the country was saved and the history of the world was changed, and this statue was raised in thanksgiving.

It is well to pause a moment and ponder the implications of the statue, for the defeat of the Persian fleet at the hands of the sea god was to have important consequences, which are still being felt. Up to this time, with brief intervals, Greece was ruled by tyrants. Having gained their freedom from a foreign tyranny, the Greeks demanded freedom for themselves, no longer obeyed their petty tyrants, and set about discovering the processes by which men can rule themselves. The statue of Poseidon celebrates the birth of freedom.

We do not know where it was erected, or what hymns were sung, or what sacrifices were offered on the day when it was unveiled for the first time. It may have stood upon a headland overlooking the waters where the Persian fleet perished, or in a temple of its own, or in the Parthenon, where Poseidon in the same attitude was represented on the west pediment. Strangely, no references to it can be found in the works of antiquity that have survived, though it is unimaginable that no one wrote about so marvelous a work. Scholars have attributed it to the sculptors Calamis, Onatas of Aegina, and Ageladas of Argos, though in the absence of comparable bronzes by these masters there can be no unanimity of opinion. Perhaps it is not important to discover the name of the sculptor, for the statue seems to have been formed, not by a single sculptor, but by the entire Greek nation, expressing all their hopes and aspirations, all their devotion to the gods, and all their sense of suddenly acquired freedom in a single act of creation at the moment of their triumph.

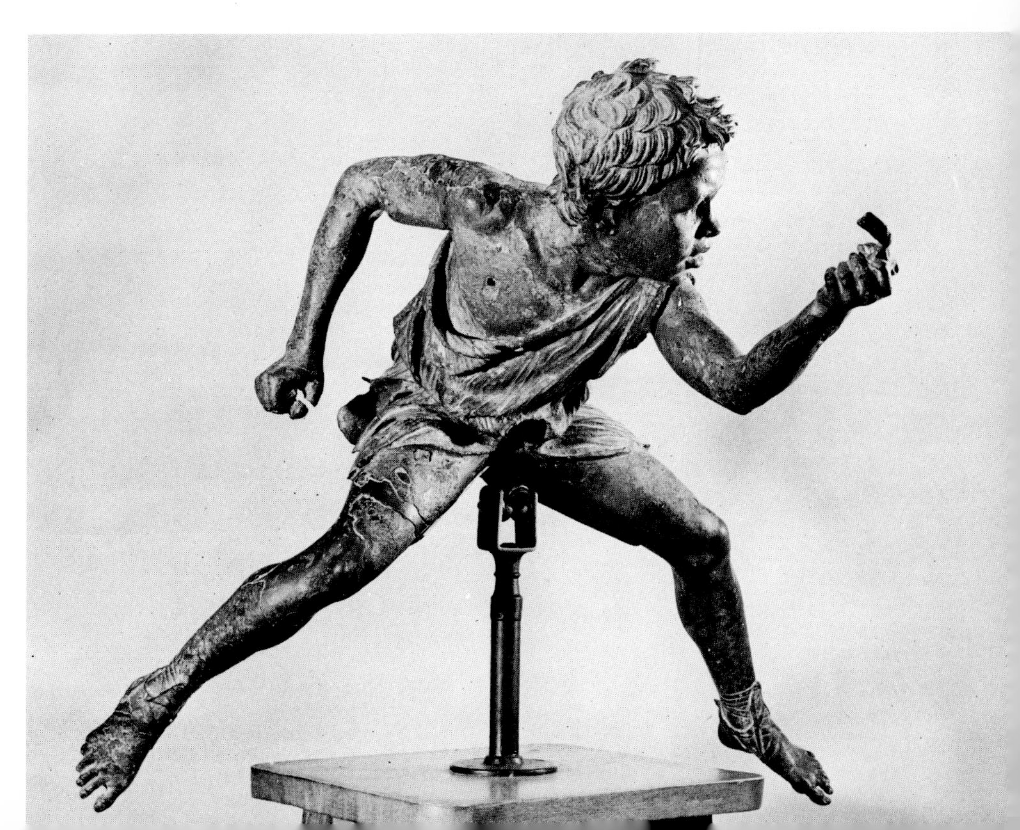

The boy rider from Artemision

What is astonishing is that the statue should have been found so close to the place where the Persian fleet was destroyed. We can almost believe that when the statue was looted by some Roman or Byzantine emperor, and carried away from Greece, Poseidon again summoned the tempest and went down into the depths which were his home.

We can scarcely hope to see greater sculpture than this, and we owe a debt to the unknown fisherman who found the left arm and set in motion the long, slow process by which the rest of the statue was found. He was not looking for blazing masterpieces. He was looking for sponges.

The archaeologists themselves are very aware of the innumerable accidents attending their profession. In the corner of the museum at Olympia there is a famous terra cotta of Zeus with a knotted stick in his hand, holding the young Ganymede under his arm. The polychrome is still vivid with its touches of blue, black, and red on the golden-brown surface. The head of this Zeus was found by German archaeologists some eighty years ago. Then it was forgotten until the chance discovery of some terra-cotta fragments in 1939, consisting of broken pieces of a torso and arm and a headless child, led to a re-examination of the head, which had been lying in a drawer. The pieces fitted, though they formed an unsatisfactory statue. The Germans continued to excavate at Olympia during the occupation of Greece. In 1942 they discovered the head of Ganymede and the lower part of Zeus. So at last the whole statue was put together from fragments collected at intervals through eighty years. Zeus proved to be strangely homely, and the rape of Ganymede shows no violence. This charming statue rather suggests a farmer carrying his young son in his arms on a market day.

The terra-cotta Zeus and Ganymede from Olympia

These accidental discoveries, these long intervals before the missing pieces are found, are the commonplaces of archaeology. No one finds what he sets out to find, the clues are innumerable and most of them are misleading; the great treasures have a habit of hiding until, of their own accord, they decide to reveal themselves. The archaeologists have learned to be patient with the treasures under the earth.

Sometimes, of course, patience is scarcely a virtue. There are even times when the archaeologist must act quickly, or not at all. A distinguished Greek archaeologist has spoken of uncovering an ancient tomb in Macedonia and seeing brilliant frescoes painted on the walls, but a moment later the frescoes disintegrated before his eyes, falling in flakes of powder. He might have had time to photograph them if he had known of their existence; might even have been able to preserve them by suddenly flooding them with a chemical fixative. Exactly the same thing sometimes happened in Crete, during the excavations at Knossos by Arthur Evans. When a fresco came to light Evans would immediately summon an artist to reproduce it quickly in water colors before the colors faded or the inevitable flaking took place. When small scraps of the fresco survived, Evans would have elaborate reconstructions made by the artist, with the result that the large wall paintings set up in the museum at Heracleion are sometimes based on only a few square inches of the original fresco. More recently, archaeologists have been using stereoscopic color cameras to record the finds immediately they are made. It seems the better, and the safer, way.

Modern technological advances are being used increasingly by archaeologists. In the old days a man went excavating with his Bible or his Homer in his hand, and his chief care was to find enough laborers, enough spades, and enough wheelbarrows so that the site could be thoroughly explored by the human ants he employed. The modern archaeologist still employs laborers, and must still go searching for spades and wheelbarrows, but he is often a technician with a knowledge of electrical resistance of the soil, aerial photography, and high-powered drills. He must be engineer, electrician, geologist, anatomist, and expert on methods of preservation—and all this in addition to being a cultural historian and the humble cub reporter asking perpetual questions of the dead. The tasks, of course, are divided, for there are few men who can embrace all the fields of archaeological knowledge. Specialization, in archaeology as in other things, can have disastrous consequences.

Mine detectors have been employed successfully in the French excavations at Entremont, where a hitherto unknown culture is being brought to light. At Gordion in central Turkey, Dr. Rodney Young of the University Museum in Philadelphia employed an oil-drilling rig to locate the tomb chamber of a Phrygian king, buried deep within a 165-foot high mound, and very similar means may soon be employed to locate the tomb chamber of Antiochus I in the almost inaccessible mound at Nemrud Dagh. In Italy the sites of innumerable Etruscan tombs have been discovered by aerial photography, and the tombs themselves have been examined by periscopic cameras sunk through the topsoil. In this way it was possible to discover whether they had been previously looted, and whether it was worth the expense of breaking into them and recovering frescoes and pottery. At Spina, at the mouth of the Po, the archaeologists manned the pumps and became hydraulic engineers, for the excavations were being made in marshlands during reclamation. Special techniques involving resistivity traverses and aerial photography are still being developed, and there would seem to be no end to the adaptations of modern techniques to archaeology. The danger is that the all-important human element may be lost in the scramble for treasure.

Archaeology is now big business. Vast sums of money are being raised to finance expeditions, and this is as it must be. Archaeology is always expensive, as Schliemann, a millionaire many times over, learned to his cost. The excavations in the Agora in Athens could not have taken place without the munificent gifts of John D. Rockefeller, Jr. But as we have seen, the most expensive undertakings are not always the most rewarding. In human and artistic terms the discovery of the bronze Poseidon off Cape Artemision was worth far more than anything discovered in the Agora, though the excavations conducted by the American School of Classical Studies were deeply rewarding. The bronze Poseidon was discovered at a cost of about $4000 in diving equipment and the life of a sponge diver. The cost of discovering the great Greek sculptured vase at Vix was no more than a few hundred francs for pumping equipment. Greek archaeologists, on salaries which would shame secretaries in America, are continually discovering objects of great value in their native country. More than one heavily financed expedition has labored to little purpose, while fishermen and farmers continue to make astounding discoveries.

Perhaps this is as it should be, for archaeology is essentially an effort to break through the boundaries of time and space in order to communicate with our ancestors, and it would be intolerable if the rich alone were granted this honor. The world of archaeology is a democracy, where the occasional tyrants are rapidly overthrown. In Israel archaeology is a popular art, practiced by students and taxi drivers, retired generals and cabinet ministers, who regard a weekend of hunting for artifacts as more rewarding than hunting for wild animals or birds. When statues from the classical period of Athens were uncovered recently just below the surface of the sidewalk at a street corner in Piraeus, the Sunday crowds came to cheer, proffering advice and claiming these statues as their own; and when Athena and Apollo and Artemis were carried off in a truck to the Piraeus Museum, the crowd followed cheering, and sometimes a strange silence descended on them. There was a feeling of awe and even of terror at the sudden prodigality of the long-dead ancients, who seemed to have chosen this time and place to reveal themselves. The crowd was grateful to the experts who took temporary possession of the statues, but no one had any illusions about the nature of their ownership. According to the normal procedure, the experts would brood over the sculptures, hide them for a few years, and write learned dissertations about them; but in the course of time they would be compelled to surrender all proprietorial rights to the people to whom they belong. Who knows or cares who first ordered them to be placed in a bath of distilled water, or who wrote the first learned paper about them? Soon enough the museum directors turn to dust, their works forgotten. The past belongs to all men, and the authority of great works of art speaks louder than the words of statesmen.

We have progressed far since the days of the ancient Romans when works of art were looted by illiterate generals to decorate their country villas. Nothing in our civilization is so healthy as our deepening respect and understanding of the people of ancient times. While we attempt to plunge deeper and deeper into space, into a violent future amid the stars, a contrary movement is taking place as we descend peacefully into the past, increasingly conscious of the wealth of our inheritance. The crowds in the museums are searching for their roots. The paperback bookshops cannot have enough books on archaeology. Expeditions set out to the remotest corners of the earth in search of vanished civilizations, to learn from the past. Thanks to the archaeologists we can look back into the earliest times, and share the joy and sadness of the individual men who created out of clay and paint and stone these monuments of our own magnificence.

Let us remember that the most important of all things is the living experience of men and women on earth; what matters most is that they should live fully. We learn soon enough that progress is an illusion, that a boy may be living more fully when riding in procession to the Parthenon than when racing a hot-rod round the neighboring streets, and that a woman dancing for the corn to grow is more alive than a woman dancing a fox-trot for no reason at all. A man in a skyscraper in Wall Street may have more primitive ideas than a man standing on the summit of a *ziggurat* in Babylon. We have learned little in ten thousand years, and we seem to have lost touch with Creation. We are beginning to realize that the ancient people of Thebes and Athens and Askelon sometimes knew more than we know.

So it is that in our own time the archaeologist has become a moralist, for he alone has the power to show us the Golden Ages, when a glory lit the heavens. He has the magic wand which gives flesh to ancient bones, and he knows the spells to summon the dead. Poseidon is discovered, and we learn the birth of freedom from a figure of awful majesty and power. The Agora is unearthed, and for the first time we can walk on the stones where democracy had its beginnings near the fish markets, the law courts, and the tomb of a hero. A German soldier brings up a stone head at Entremont, and we learn years later that the ancestors of the French were head-hunters. At Gordion in central Turkey we discover designs which are so characteristically European that we can no longer believe that Europe starts at the Hellespont. At Cyrene in North Africa we find the ruins of a city more majestic than our own. In the end we learn that we are the inheritors of traditions greater than ourselves.

More and more we are realizing that the past is all around us, and we have only to pick it up to make it our own. As we learn to examine our own beliefs and customs in the light of beliefs and customs held long ago, we sometimes discover that the ancients solved problems which still bedevil us. We used to think of ourselves as the descendants of the Greeks and the Romans, and so we are, but now we are beginning to know that the Greeks and Romans were the children of an ancient family. Beyond them there used to be ghostly figures in the twilight. Now we see them in the full light of the ancient sun.

Today, when we summon the past, it comes running into our arms.

## III

In the future, what can we expect to find? What treasures remain to be discovered? Where should we look? Are we at the beginning of new horizons in archaeology, or are we coming to the end?

This book, though it deals only with recent discoveries around the Mediterranean lake, is designed to show that we have scarcely begun. Whole empires, entire cities, remain to be discovered. A thousand Greek statues lie at the bottom of the sea, and in the last sixty years scarcely a dozen have been brought to the surface. Whole libraries remain to be discovered, for it is unthinkable that we have lost forever the unknown works of Sappho, Aeschylus, and Sophocles. As the archaeologists grow more cunning, and the spades dig deeper, we can expect to find more treasures than we ever hoped for. There is more treasure under the earth than over it; and the gold vessels slumbering in the darkness have not long to wait before they see the sun again.

Cities under the sea will be brought to light once more; we shall track the unknown roads where the ancients traveled, and find their lodging houses; from there we shall go on to uncover their market places, and the towns on the ancient frontiers where the cultures met, and by meeting invigorated one another. Large areas of North Africa, Turkey, and Central Europe remain to be explored. Homer proclaimed that Crete had ninety cities; only seven or eight have been discovered, and only two or three have been thoroughly excavated, although Crete stands in a position of sovereign eminence in the history of Europe. Sicily, too, deserves to be regarded with a special affection, for there are half a dozen Greek cities in Sicily which have vanished from the maps and never been excavated.

For centuries Greek culture was the strongest civilizing influence in the Mediterranean, and therefore we can expect that for many years to come archaeology around the Mediterranean will be concerned with the exploration of Greek civilization on the shores of Europe and Africa. More than two thirds of the discoveries described in the present book are directly or indirectly connected with Greece, and it could hardly be otherwise. I have begun with the Greek treasures found near Paris in 1951, and then by way of Italy, Yugoslavia, Greece, Turkey, Israel, and Cyrenaica circled the Mediterranean to end in the small village of Haidra where Tunisian workmen in 1939 found a wonderful mosaic made by

Africans in a style which is wholly Greek. Nearly all the treasures described here were found in the last thirty years.

The Greeks themselves were too busy producing great works of art to feel very keenly about the past. For them time was the enemy, and they ached for the lost beauty, but made little effort to recapture it. We hear of a few sporadic archaeological expeditions in ancient Greece, but nothing much came of them. The Greek attitude towards the shadowy world of their ancestors is expressed in one of Lucian's *Dialogues of the Dead*, where Hermes is interrogated by Menippos:

MENIPPOS Where are all the beauties, Hermes? Please show me around, for I am a newcomer.

HERMES I am busy, Menippos. But if you look to your right, you will see Hyacinth, Narcissos, Niraeus, Achilles, Tyro, Helen and Leda—all the beauties of ancient days.

MENIPPOS I see only bones and skulls, and nearly all of them are exactly alike.

HERMES Those bones, which you dismiss so lightly, have been sung by adoring poets.

MENIPPOS Fair enough, but show me Helen. Myself, I wouldn't be able to distinguish her from all the others.

HERMES Here is Helen's skull.

MENIPPOS Is that the skull for which a thousand ships carried warriors from every corner of Greece, and Greeks and barbarians were slain, and cities were made desolate?

HERMES Oh, Menippos, you never saw the living Helen, or you would have said with Homer:

Well might they suffer grievous years of toil,
Who strove for such a prize.

We look at withered flowers when all the color's gone from them, and do we not say they are unlovely things. So, too, in the hour of their flowering these skulls were lovely.

We are luckier than the ancient Greeks, for we know more about their ancestors than they ever knew, and we can almost clothe the ancient bones with flesh and give life to them. The conquest of the past has begun. Of all our conquests this may be the most enduring.

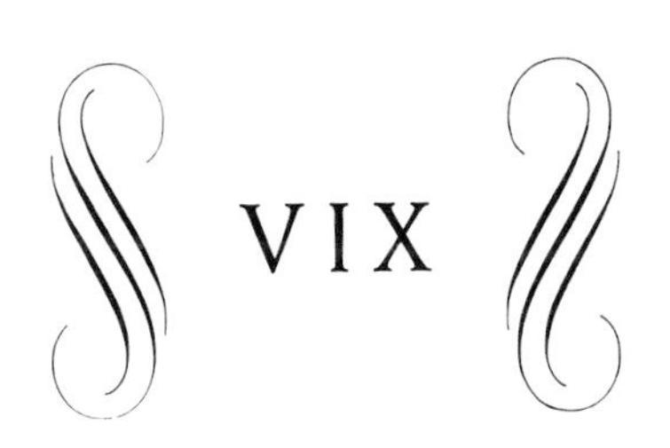

# VIX

ABOUT a hundred miles southeast of Paris, in the rolling Burgundian countryside, lies the small red-roofed hamlet of Vix in the shadow of a low, pine-clad hill called Mont Lassois. Vix is so small a place that it is rarely marked on a map, but to archaeologists Mont Lassois was known as the site of a fortified town dating from about 800 B.C. Judging by the enormous number of pottery fragments found there, the hill had once supported a population of a thousand people. Traces of ramparts and a wide moat were discovered; the hill-fort evidently commanded the headwaters of the river Seine, which winds tortuously past the hill. The excavations of Mont Lassois, begun in 1929, were chiefly of interest to specialists in the Bronze and Iron Ages. No treasure was found. A few pearls, a few brooches, and more than a million fragments of pottery—such were the fruits of almost ten years' patient work by the archaeologists.

Outside the pages of learned archaeological journals Vix would have been completely forgotten if it had not been for an extraordinary series of accidents. The war in France effectively ended in 1940, and René Joffroy, a young professor of philosophy, was demobilized and sent to teach in a school at Châtillon-sur-Seine, three miles south of Vix. Joffroy was a small, chubby, good-humored man with a passion for archaeology. He went to Châtillon-sur-Seine as a replacement, expecting to stay there for only three months, but in fact he stayed for seventeen years. He taught school, collected insects—for he was an amateur entomologist—and took charge of the local excavations. He was fascinated by Mont Lassois and continued to dig on the hill without finding anything of great importance.

Meanwhile he had come to various definite conclusions. Although the hill had revealed little more than an enormous, unmanageable pile of pottery fragments, it became clear to him that the fortified town must have played an increasingly important role in the history of the region until about the sixth century B.C., when it was at the height of its power. Thereafter there was a long, slow decline. He felt certain that important sixth-century relics would be found. He drew up a memorandum to the Historical Monuments Commission in 1951, insisting on the importance of excavations at Mont Lassois, and was rewarded with a small grant. Digging went on through all of 1952. Nothing was found.

One day towards the end of the year René Joffroy fell into conversation with Maurice Moisson, a peasant smallholder and gravedigger from Vix, who had often worked for him. Moisson, whose name means "harvest," was a lean, handsome man with a narrow, sunburned face and a shock of dark hair, possessed of a grave courtesy and dignity. Together they lamented the year's failure. They had hoped to find the tombs of the ancient rulers of Mont Lassois, or some important relics—a temple, a treasury—but they were as far away as ever from finding any clues, and the season was nearly over, with only a few francs remaining from the grant. Then the lightning struck.

Maurice Moisson remembered that on the field next to his own there was a broad scattering of stones which could have come only from a distant quarry, and that there was a scarcely perceptible hump in the earth where the stones lay. Was it possible that these stones had once formed part of a tumulus over a grave? Was it possible that the tombs of the ancient rulers of the hill-fortress might be on the plain and not on the hill? Joffroy agreed that it was possible, though unlikely, and they went to examine the site. There was the broad field with the hump in it, and the stones scattered far and wide. The permission of the owner was secured, and Moisson set to digging.

So the digging began. It was January, the weather freezing, bitter winds coming over the plains. On the evening of January 3, 1953, René Joffroy went back to Châtillon-sur-Seine, while Moisson went on digging until it was nearly dark. He could not have told why he went on digging, or why he had selected this precise spot. Darkness was falling fast when his spade rang against some metal object. It was heavy, curiously curved, covered with earth, and frozen into the ground. He pulled, but he could not detach it. Puzzled, he wandered back along the narrow path to his

The great Wine Vessel of Vix

house at the corner of the village street, and early the next morning he was on his way to Châtillon-sur-Seine to see René Joffroy.

"I don't know what it is," Moisson said. "It's big and heavy, and seems to be made of bronze. I'd say it looks like a mule's packsaddle."

"How big is it?"

Moisson spread out his hands.

"That big?"

"Yes, and there's more of it below the earth."

René Joffroy had four hours of teaching that morning. The time passed slowly—far too slowly for any comfort. But at noon he got into his small car and drove to Vix, where he saw immediately that there was in fact something which resembled a mule's packsaddle. What he saw was the heavily ornamented double handle of an enormous Greek wine vessel. The type of handle was well known, but no one had ever seen a handle so large, so heavy, so sculptural. It was as though the arm of a giant were slowly lifting up through the earth.

There followed days of intense and exhausting labor, in near-freezing weather. Rain fell, the earth was waterlogged, and pumps were brought in. René Joffroy realized they had come upon a burial chamber about twelve feet square, where once there had been wooden posts at the four corners and a wooden roof, with heavy stones protecting the roof. The wood had decayed; the stones had fallen into the burial chamber and crushed everything below.

The enormous wine vessel—the largest and most sumptuous ever found—was not badly damaged. The base had broken off, and there were rents and cracks in its great bellying bowl, but it was otherwise intact. This was the first object to emerge from the ground, and it was quickly followed by others. With scrupulous care each object was photographed as soon as it was uncovered.

The wine vessel, or *krater*, proved to be five feet high, weighing a quarter of a ton, and holding, if wine had ever been poured into it, more than a thousand liters of wine. But what were most remarkable were the procession of ingeniously carved bronze horses, with their naked but helmeted attendants forming a frieze around the rim of the vessel, and the beautiful and complex Gorgons, grimacing and poking out their tongues, which were sculptured into the highly decorative handles. This wine vessel was in fact a sophisticated work of art, and even at first glance, when covered with mud, it appeared to derive from the greatest period of Greek metalwork. Such a vessel could only have belonged to a king.

The diadem surrounding the broken skull, photographed during excavations at Vix

There was more—much more—to come. Soon there was found, quite close to the wine vessel, the pathetic remains of a woman, who had apparently been lying on the floor of a funeral cart, surrounded by gifts and offerings. to accompany her on her journey to the next world. There was a heavy gold diadem round her head, a bronze bracelet round her neck, and bronze rings round her ankles. The bones were crushed, and only the skull had survived the fall of the roof beams and the shower of stones. Judging by the teeth, it was the skull of a woman between thirty and thirty-five years old, and to some extent the features could be reconstructed: A high broad forehead, a straight nose, heavy cheekbones. She was longheaded, and probably came of Celtic stock. There was evidence of a wound which had suppurated for some time; and from this wound she had probably died.

A winged horse from the diadem

The gold diadem was the second marvel to come out of the burial chamber. It weighed more than a pound, and was gracefully and wonderfully curved, while the ends were formed of lions' paws gripping globes of amazing intricacy with two minute winged horses galloping off the globes. These winged horses were no larger than a fingernail, but the artist had given them the breath of life, marking the hairs of the horses' coats and the feathers of the horses' wings. With incredible delicacy and precision he had woven a thick gold carpet for them. The base of each globe was carved into delicate concentric circles of filigree, and these circles seem to suggest ever-widening rings of power. These little horses are completely mysterious. Nothing like them had ever been found before. They seem to go back to the ancestors of the present-day horses which once ranged the steppes of Russia; and their origin is perhaps Scythian.

The gold diadem of Vix

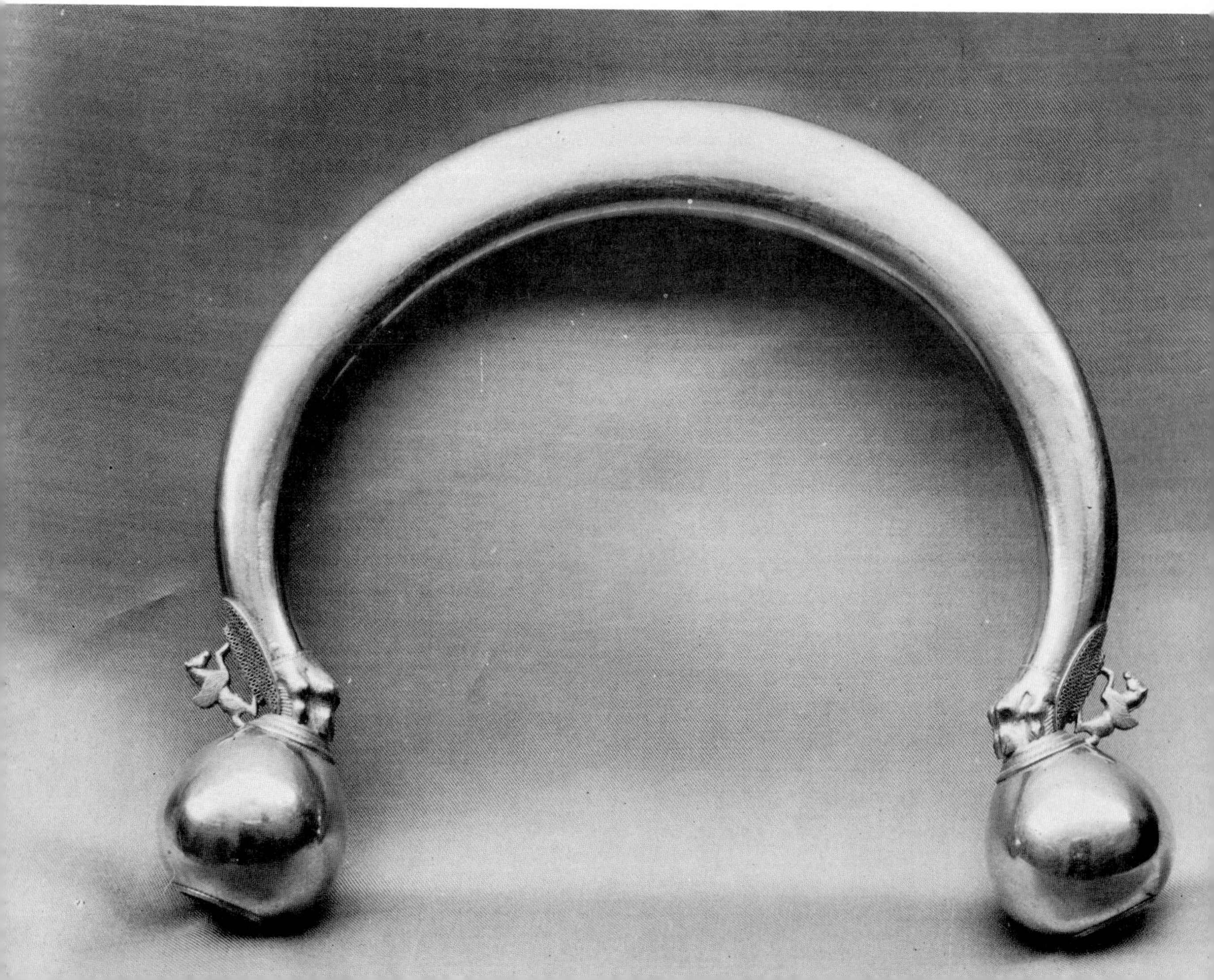

Nearby were found the usual utensils for cooking food and mixing wine, amulets and amber necklaces, a Greek vase of the two-handled type called a Droop cup decorated in red and black with a scene of Greek warriors fighting Amazons, and the remnants of the cart in sufficient number to enable the archaeologists to reconstruct it. The wheels were about two and a half feet in diameter, and each had eight spokes. Some bronze plaques like horse brasses were also found. The lid of the great *krater* was also found, decorated with the statue of a goddess about six inches high in a style so different from the running horses and naked warriors on the majestic frieze that it could be confidently assumed that it came from another workshop altogether. The goddess is molded with the peculiar smoothness associated with sculptures from the island of Samos.

The processional frieze from the great Wine Vessel of Vix

There were many other small objects in the burial chamber: fibulae, rings, small vases, a bronze ewer, Greek pottery, a silver cup: but none of these can be compared with the golden diadem and the enormous wine vessel for beauty or rarity. These staggered the imagination, and it was not easy to understand how they had come to this field so close to Paris. When? By what routes? For what purpose? Why were they placed in the tomb of a Celtic princess who had apparently died in battle?

The Droop cup with the Greek warriors fighting the Amazons provides a terminal date, for it is the style of the cups painted in Athens between 530 and 520 B.C., and these dates are in fair agreement with the style of the decoration on the wine vessel, where the archaic stiffness is giving way to quick and electric movement. Thirty-two horses, eight charioteers, and seven foot soldiers are depicted on the vessel. It has been suggested that the foot soldiers represent the seven heroes who marched against Thebes, but it is just as likely that they represent any triumphal procession. These figures are not stamped out: They are all carved separately, and each has its own special characteristics. One soldier leans forward a little more than another; some have beards while others are beardless. There are subtle differences between the horses, and each chariot and charioteer is conceived separately and distinctively. The effect is to suggest a formal procession marching in full vigor before a king. It is a demonstration of strength. The foot soldiers wear helmets with flowing plumes, they carry shields, and there are greaves on their legs; but there are no swords or spears. None of them is armed. What is represented is naked power, the power which has no need of weapons.

The Droop Cup from the tomb chamber of the princess

This extraordinary frieze is a thing to ponder on, for it is among the great surviving works of Greek art. The very shape of the *krater* speaks of authority and what the French call *plénitude,* and this authority is immeasurably increased by the controlled violence of the frieze. The *krater* is evidently not an Athenian work. Judging by similar figures of foot soldiers found in Sparta, the frieze can confidently be ascribed to a Spartan workshop.

By what strange hazard, we may ask, did a great Spartan wine vessel bearing on its cover the statue of a Samian goddess reach a cabbage field in France?

This was a problem which exercised the mind of René Joffroy until he could almost cry out with the wonder and agony of the discovery. There was, however, one breathtaking clue in the pages of the historian Herodotus. Was it possible—was it conceivable—that this wine vessel was the one which, according to Herodotus, the Spartans offered to the rich and miserly King Croesus in 546 B.C. in return for the many favors he had shown them? As Herodotus tells the story, the great *krater* was already on its way to the Lydian court when Croesus was attacked and made prisoner by King Cyrus of Persia. The ship bearing the gift was sailing near Samos, off the coast of Asia Minor, when it was attacked by Samian pirates who removed the vessel and carried it off to the shrine of their patron goddess. Here is Herodotus' story:

> The Spartans prepared themselves to come at the summons of King Croesus, and not content with this, they fashioned an enormous bronze vase, large enough to hold 300 *amphorae* and covered with figures of living creatures around the outside of the rim, and they sent this vase to Croesus in return for the gifts he had given them, but for some reason the vase never reached Sardis. There are two quite different stories about the fate of the vase. One story says that somewhere off Samos the islanders got wind of the presence of the vase, put to sea in their warships and made off with the prize; that at any rate is the story told by the Spartans. The Samians however tell another story. According to them, the Spartans arrived too late, and hearing that Sardis had fallen and Croesus was a prisoner, they sold it to the islanders, and the purchasers (who were private citizens) placed it as an offering in the Temple of Hera.

> And indeed, if they sold it, it is likely enough that on their return to Sparta they would pretend they had been robbed by the Samians. So much for the story of the vase.

Such was the story told by Herodotus, and René Joffroy, when writing his official report on the discovery, could not prevent himself from pointing out the strange likeness of the Vix *krater* and the vase described by Herodotus. What would be more likely than that the Samians on taking possession of the vase would crown it with the figure of their own goddess? If the soldiers were unarmed, that could be explained by the nature of the gift honoring the alliance between Sparta and Lydia. There was no doubt of the Spartan workmanship, and Herodotus had clearly indicated that the Spartans had fashioned it themselves. The pieces of the jigsaw were fitting together almost too neatly.

A Gorgon from the handle of the Wine Vessel

We may never know how the *krater* came to France, nor why it was placed in the burial chamber of a Celtic princess. Samos suffered from a succession of violent revolutions, and the Temple of Hera was plundered many times. Pirates could have stolen the treasure and taken it by sea to the Greek colony at Marseilles, whence it could easily have been transported up the Rhône. Or it may have traveled by way of Italy through the Alpine passes and so to the high valleys of the Rhône and the Rhine, following the roads taken by the Argonauts in their search of the Golden Fleece. In the *Argonautica* Apollonius of Rhodes describes how they passed by "the stormy lakes which stretch into the Celtic country," a reference probably to the Swiss lakes, and went unhindered "through the numerous tribes of the Celts." Vix may have been a Celtic stronghold commanding the portages from the Seine to the Rhône, levying a tax on Baltic amber and British tin, growing rich and powerful as a frontier trading post. How rich and powerful it must have been we know from the wealth poured into the tomb of the Celtic princess.

Today, the treasure of Vix is assembled in a room especially built for it in the museum at Châtillon-sur-Seine. Not even a color photograph can suggest the richness of the texture of the *krater,* or the glowing patina which is the result of 2,500 years of immersion in the earth. When I saw it, the sun was blazing through the windows, and it was the color and shape of purple grapes. Standing on a polished wooden pedestal, it stood as high as a man. I have never seen any other object made by human hands which gives such an impression of human majesty.

Maurice Moisson took me over the field where it had been found. It was a cold, blustery day, with threads of gossamer lying over the plowed furrows, and there were still multitudes of stones like marble chips on the earth. Nine feet underground had lain the Celtic princess, the purple vase and the golden diadem. I asked him what he felt when he saw the treasure coming out of the ground.

"Joy," he answered. "The purest joy imaginable. *Voyez-vous,* such things do not happen many times in the life of a man."

Samian goddess from the cover of the Wine Vessel of Vix

Life-sized statue of a seated god from Entremont

# ENTREMONT

UNTIL recently little was known about the art of the ancient Gauls. Occasionally there would be found a hoard of Gallic coins, the design stamped on them resembling coins of ancient Greece, but with the features violently distorted into fierce free-flowing abstractions. A few carved Gallic reliefs survived, the most important being an altar found in 1711 under the choir of Nôtre Dame, with portraits of the gods carved on it—Cernunnos, a ferocious monster with horns springing out of his head, Esus the brawny god of the woodlands bearing in his hand the small hatchet with which he cropped the sacred mistletoe. The pantheon of the Gauls was very large, and we know the names of several hundred of their gods. Some of their strange customs are recorded by ancient Greek and Roman authors, but the people themselves remained curiously baffling. We did not know how they saw themselves.

In 1943 some Germans occupying a radio transmitting post on a small hill overlooking Aix-en-Provence in the south of France dug a well. Some fragments of statues were found, and with them a curious relief of a dead man's head by a practiced but primitive hand.

This was not the first time Gallic remains had been found on the hill at Entremont. In 1817 some theological students on an afternoon stroll came upon a death's-head carved on a pillar; they reported their find, and the pillar was removed to the museum of Aix where it was forgotten until the novelist Prosper Mérimée, the author of *Carmen* and at the time an inspector of historical monuments, saw it and noted in his travel-diary: "It must have been made by the Saluvii, for only they could have done it so badly." At long intervals more statues were discovered. In 1877 a relief showing a cluster of four death's-heads joined the pillar in the Aix museum. They were not great works of art, they were oddly disturbing, and were soon forgotten.

Why they should have been forgotten so quickly is something of a puzzle, for the history of the hill at Entremont was well known. On this hill there were once palaces, temples, ramparts, a sacred way; there were treasuries and armories; and a king issued orders which were obeyed as far as the Swiss mountains and the Pyrenees. It was the sacred city of the Saluvii, a Celtic tribe which played a leading role in a confederation of tribes occupying most of southern France. In 124 B.C. the Saluvii, under their king Teutomalius, attacked the Greek settlement in Marseilles, then under the protection of the Romans. In the following year the Roman general Caius Sextius Calvinus took his terrible revenge. The city on the hill was attacked by an overwhelming force armed with stone-throwing catapults. Orders were given that the city should be utterly destroyed with no stone left standing on another. Teutomalius was able to escape, but most of the defenders were killed and the survivors sold into slavery. The statues of the gods were hurled down, and the city razed to the ground. A new town, the first Roman town in Gaul, was built in the valley below. It was called *Aquae Sextiae*, "the waters of Sextius," and this ancient Roman name has been corrupted into the modern Aix.

Few cities have ever been completely destroyed. The hill city of the Saluvii was sacked, the columns of the temples were pulled down, the stone walls of the houses were battered into rubble, and no one was allowed to live on the desolate hill; but the broken gods lay where they fell. In time grass and trees covered them, and the ancient city was forgotten. But even in the Middle Ages the hill was regarded with awe, and fables were told of a king's head made entirely of gold which was buried somewhere in the hill, and of a golden goat, symbol of fertility, which would one day spring out of the hill's side.

The Germans were the first serious archaeologists at Entremont. After digging the well and discovering the fragments of statues and the death's-head, they dug several trenches and brought to light a few more pieces of sculpture all marked by the peculiarly heavy, rough-hewn Gallic style. Fernand Benoit, a French archaeologist then living at Aix, heard of these discoveries and appealed successfully to the Germans to leave them in the museum for further study. As soon as the war was over, he obtained funds and began the serious excavation of the hill. Unfortunately, the Ministry of War refused to abandon its radio signal station, and the excavators were allowed to work on a small part of the hill only.

The excavations at Entremont are among the most important in modern France, but no one walking up the hill and seeing the site of the excavations, which is about the size of a French potato field, would realize that this small strip of earth had profoundly changed our knowledge of ancient Gaul. There are a few roads, a few remnants of walls two or three feet high, and almost hidden among pine trees are some great fortification walls, stones piled on stones. But it was here, in a small sanctuary, that Fernand Benoit found the broken statues and the portrait heads and the curious lintels with hollows scooped out to hold the skulls of the enemies of the Gauls, which are now in the museum at Aix. For the first time it became possible to see the ancient Gauls as they saw themselves.

Relief of decapitated heads from Entremont

The Greek author Poseidonius, the friend of Cicero, born about ten years before the fall of the hill city of the Saluvii, remembered seeing human skulls nailed to the walls. He said, too, that victorious Gallic chieftains wore human skulls hanging from their necks on strings. He remarked quietly, as though it were a fact well known to everyone, that they were head-hunters. With the excavations at Entremont it became clear that the Saluvii practiced the cult of the death's-head. Human skulls were found with nails driven through them. Carved crudely, but with extraordinary power, were the representations of dead enemies—

sometimes singly, sometimes in twos, sometimes in clusters of four. Occasionally miniature heads to the number of about twenty are carved on a single stone lintel.

There were also representations of living heads, and these were evidently the portraits of chieftains. Some wore leather helmets, others wore diadems. All were broken, and they lay among the heavy stones thrown from Roman catapults just as they had fallen in 123 B.C. All these portraits and death's-heads are marked by an austere and savage power. The Gallic artists were demonstrably influenced by Greek sculptures, which they had probably seen in Marseilles, but they have their own particular vision, their own conception of how to shape and bring life to the stone.

Take, for example, the head of the woman being held in the grip of a powerful hand. The artist has represented a head as seen in a moment of visionary horror, not the head of a dead person. He has given overwhelming strength to the widely spaced fingers, and these too are fingers seen in the lightning-flash of horror. Or take the chieftain's portrait with the curls matted close to the skull. His head has been broken and the nose is damaged, but it is a recognizable portrait of a type which still exists in France: long face, clear forehead, thin lips, jutting jaw. But where the artist is most successful is in giving a sense of high seriousness, of deep thought behind the high forehead. He is a man who ponders, who knows where he is going, and who is inflexible in his purposes; he would make a good administrator or a good engineer.

Hand holding a decapitated head from Entremont

Then there is the life-size figure of a warrior sitting cross-legged, wearing a tightly fitting leather coat with a medallion of a lion's head on his breast. He is headless, armless, legless, but we are aware of the breath of life flowing in his capacious chest. From other similar statues we know that he was not a warrior, but a god, holding a thunderbolt in one hand and a death's-head in the other. Power streams from him. Even in his mutilated state he gives an impression of calm majesty.

The excavations at Entremont are incomplete. We shall know a good deal more about the ancient Gauls when the Ministry of War abandons the hill to the archaeologists. But even with the present discoveries, we are able to see the ancient Gauls as they were: more savage and ruthless than we ever guessed. Writing at about the time of Christ the geographer Strabo said they were "war-mad, high-spirited, eager for battle, and in other respects simple and not uncultivated." He was saying no more than the truth.

As you walk down from the hill at Entremont toward the red roofs of Aix, you pass a white house set a little apart from the road. This house is the studio of Cézanne on the Chemin de Lauves, where he painted during the last years of his life. He often painted on Entremont, looking out toward his beloved Mont Sainte Victoire. On entering the studio you will find seven brown skulls arranged on a shelf, and seeing those skulls which he often painted, you will find yourself wondering at the curiously long-lived tradition of the French with respect to the human head. The ancient Gauls were head-hunters and nailed heads on their walls as signs of their prowess. In the Middle Ages the severed heads appear again on the capitals of churches. Then came the guillotine, the mechanical head-hunter. For the French, even today, the head is the seat of the soul and of the intelligence. Entremont throws light on the French, as the French themselves throw light on the ancient Gauls.

The Sacred Way at Glanum

# GLANUM

WHEN in the last months of his life Vincent van Gogh was living in an asylum at Saint-Rémy, the doctor would sometimes permit him to take his easel into the nearby fields. On such days he would always keep close to the asylum and usually he would turn towards the strange, tormented mountains called the Alpilles and paint them furiously, with perhaps a stretch of cornfield in the foreground and a solitary reaper moving mysteriously into the distance. Cézanne, painting at Entremont, did not know that there was a city of the head-hunters under his feet, and Vincent van Gogh never knew there was a marble city only twenty feet below his paintbrush.

The discovery of the city of Glanum is due largely to the work of the archaeologist Henri Rolland, but it might never have been discovered at all if Louis Ibis had not been walking his dog just outside Saint-Rémy one day shortly after World War I. Louis Ibis was an elderly Frenchman who had spent his life as a cashier in the Galeries Lafayette department store in Paris. A careful man, he had invested his money carefully—in Russian bonds. When the war came to an end he was ruined, and his dream of spending his declining years in a small property in the south of France seemed to be unattainable. Nevertheless, with almost no money he settled in Saint-Rémy, famous for two thousand years for its triumphal arch and the wonderfully delicate and intricate mausoleum erected in honor of the grandsons of Augustus Caesar. The arch and the mausoleum lie close to one another in a small sunken garden outside the town. Louis Ibis needed to supplement his income, and he asked permission to be the local guide. He would take visitors to the two monuments and discuss them with learning and humor, and he was grateful for the tips. Usually he was accompanied by a small dog. One day when he was wandering on the low foothills just beyond the monuments, a stone's throw from Vincent van Gogh's asylum, he saw the dog scratching on some white stones half hidden in the bushes. These white stones proved to be the top of a building. The discovery of Glanum had begun.

Over the years many trenches were dug and many buildings came to light, but it was only in 1942 that a determined effort was made to plan the excavation of the entire city. In that year Henri Rolland, a numismatist with a vast knowledge of ancient Greece and Rome, settled in Saint-Rémy on his return from a German prison camp. He knew a great deal about the excavations which had been carried on halfheartedly for twenty years, and he had already developed some general theories about the site. Funds, always inadequate, were set aside for the new excavations. During the following twenty years most of the city was brought to light.

Like Entremont, Glanum was a sacred city, owing its sanctity to the sweet waters of a spring high up on the hillside. Like Entremont, too, it had been sacked and then abandoned and almost completely forgotten. But in every other respect Glanum is entirely unlike Entremont. It is a Greek city, with temples and porticoes and altars set up in open spaces. It was built by Greeks, perhaps from the Greek colony at Marseilles, on the foundations of an ancient Gallic city, and in time it became a Roman holiday resort. It is the only city in France which bears the imprint of Gallic, Greek, and Roman influences. The Greek influence is dominant. As you wander through these ghostly white streets, you have the strange feeling that you will shortly turn a corner and see Athens in the distance. You wonder what a Greek city is doing here under the burning skies of southern France.

Yet there is very little mystery about Glanum. Though forgotten for centuries, it had a reputable history and was frequently mentioned by ancient authors. Long ago it had been suspected that the triumphal arch was probably the gateway to a city which had vanished in some unaccountable way. What had happened was very simple. Rain had brought the detritus of the hills down over the city like a lava-flow, and it had vanished like Herculaneum and Pompeii.

Today the history of Glanum can be mapped out in considerable detail. At first it seems to have been a frontier trading post between the Greek colony in the south of France and the Gallic tribes to the north. Under the Greek name of Glanon—it became Glanum under the Roman

Gallo-Roman head found at Glanum in 1952

An acroterium from Glanum

occupation—it minted its own coins and levied its own taxes. We know that Gauls came to live within its walls because they left Gallic inscriptions written in the Greek alphabet, and also some characteristic Gallic portrait heads, not unlike those unearthed at Entremont. One of these heads, unearthed at Glanum in 1952, depicts a long-haired Gallic chieftain whose features derive at a great distance from the Greek *kouroi*. The face is deeply pitted, but the nobility of the expression is still discernible. Gallic, too, is the three-horned bull with the sweeping tail and the oddly pompous stance, seething with power though only two inches long. The sleeping Negro boy, with his head lying on his left hand, comes however from a workshop in Alexandria, and though not much larger than the bull, he too is powerfully depicted. There is a studied ruthlessness in the delineation of the boy's features, half caricature, half affectionate portrait; and if by some miracle the boy were to come running into the room, you would recognize him. Greek, too, are the acroteria, the flowering scrolls which decorated the roofs of buildings, here supported on the back of the goddess Valetudo, whose features are damaged, though some of her purposefulness comes through her broken face. Eight or nine of these vast acroteria have been found at Glanum, and they are among the chief glories of the new museum at Saint-Rémy, which has been built to house the discoveries at Glanum and all the other relics of the countryside. They once rose from the roofs of buildings like gifts of flowers, more florid than the tight stone bouquets on the temples in Greece. Some Gallic roughness adheres to them. Those heavily curving leaves suggest that Gaul could sometimes influence Greece.

Until the final conquest of Gaul by Julius Caesar, Glanum seems to have retained its predominantly Greek character. Then gradually the Romans began to assume a more important position in the life of the city. We hear of visits to the city by Augustus Caesar and by Marcus Agrippa, who married Caesar's daughter Julia; and the only known portrait head of Julia was discovered in 1951 in an abandoned well in Glanum by Henri Rolland, who recognized her features because they are stamped on coins. She gave Agrippa three sons and two daughters, but on her husband's death abandoned herself to adulteries and was banished by her father. The portrait conveys her proud willfulness and her stylish hair-do. Two of her children who died young, Gaius and Lucius, are commemorated in the great mausoleum which lies just outside Glanum.

The bust of Julia, daughter of Augustus, from Glan

In time, Glanum became a favorite watering place for rich Romans traveling in Gaul. The first and second centuries A.D. saw it at the height of its prosperity, no longer a frontier trading post but a city which existed in its own right. People came to drink the waters of the sacred spring, mounting the ornamental steps leading up the hillside. The white city with its ample streets looks parched today, but in Greek and Roman times it must have been gay with flowers and green with trees watered by trickling streams. The rich and the fashionable wandered through those shady streets, and one of the richest dropped a crystal ring carved with her own portrait. She wears the hair-do which was fashionable in the time of the Emperor Trajan, with heavy waves piled on top of one another. Oddly, she seems to mimic the pompous shape and energy of the three-horned bull.

Bronze bull from Glanum

Crystal ring of the late first century A.D., found at Glanum

Glanum's wealth can be measured by the number of temples. There were temples and altars to more than a dozen gods and goddesses, but the greater worship seems to have been offered to Cybele, "the Great Mother," beloved by the shepherd Atys, who suffered ingloriously when he proved unfaithful to her. A charming relief found at Glanum shows him reclining in the shade of a palm tree, his gown swirling in the summer wind, his Phrygian cap askew, one hand resting on his cheek and the other hiding his lost masculinity. He lies on a bed of flowers, dreaming his life away.

So it may have been with Glanum herself, the rich and flowering city on the hillside, beloved by Augustus Caesar. There were no heavy ramparts, no fortifications, and only a small garrison. One day, about the year A.D. 270, a barbarian tribe came over the hills and sacked the city, and the city died. These barbarians were probably the mysterious Herulians who sacked Athens a few years earlier, doing their work well. Then for nearly seventeen hundred years the city lay in its grave, waiting until Henri Rolland brought it once again to life.

The relief of Atys from Glanum

The Ganymede from Sperlonga

# SPERLONGA

At this time a dangerous accident occurred to the Emperor, increasing the vague rumors about him, and giving him greater confidence in the friendship and loyalty of Sejanus. They were dining in a villa called "The Cave," in a natural cave between the Gulf of Amyclae and the hills of Fundi. Suddenly at the cave-mouth there was a rock-fall, and several servants were crushed to death. Panic seized the whole company, and the diners fled. Sejanus, however, braced himself across the Emperor on hands and knees, keeping off the falling boulders; and so they were found when the soldiers came to rescue them.

SUCH is the strange story told by Tacitus in his *Annals*, and it may be remarked that Sejanus was capable of anything—even engineering a rock-fall. It would not have been too difficult. The cave itself was a marvel of artificiality, with fountains, pools, watercourses, and innumerable statues, many of them carved out of the living rock. Sejanus could well have arranged that rocks should fall at a signal, taking care that only a few pebbles should fall on the table where he was dining with the Emperor; and the loss of a few servants at the cave's mouth was a small price to pay for the favor of his imperial master. When Tiberius was in his dotage, Sejanus became Emperor in everything except name until Tiberius grew suspicious and had him executed.

The cave between the Gulf of Amyclae and the hills of Fundi has long been known, but no one seriously excavated there until the summer of 1957 when Erno Bellante, a highway engineer working on a nearby stretch of coastal road, decided to explore it. He was an amateur archaeologist with a considerable knowledge of ancient Roman history. What he found after a few days' work exceeded his wildest dreams. Under a thick carpet of fallen rocks lay a great jumble of marble fragments: arms, legs, torsos. Professor Giulio Jacopi, the Superintendent of Antiquities in the Roman area, was working on the foundations of a Roman villa not far away, and he was hastily summoned. The Roman villa was thereupon forgotten, and in the space of a few weeks the archaeologists uncovered more than 5,000 fragments of sculpture in the cave.

The exploration of the cave itself was an arduous undertaking, for many reasons. In the first place, almost no money was available, but this difficulty was overcome when Erno Bellante offered his own private funds to the archaeologists. In the second place, the cave was continually being flooded by springs, and so three pumps were set to work. Then huge quantities of ammunition and high explosives, stored there since World War II, threatened to blow up the entire cave. An ordnance expert was summoned, and kept constantly on duty. Finally, as soon as they became aware of the importance of the discovery, the people of the neighboring town of Sperlonga (from the Latin *spelunca,* "a cave") threatened to create trouble if a single piece of the statuary was removed to Rome. They wanted the cave transformed into a local museum, in this way enticing tourists to their town. The archaeologists wanted to take the fragments to Rome for further study. The townspeople threatened to blow up the cave by shooting into the ammunition dump, and they dug ditches across the road leading to the cave. This war between Sperlonga and the archaeologists ended with the arrival of the police, but the bitterness remained.

The mouth of the cave at Sperlonga

Among the first pieces discovered were giant-sized limbs, including a leg seven feet long corresponding to a figure nearly twenty feet high, the fragments of two colossal snakes, two life-sized torsos, and a mutilated Greek inscription reading: "Athenodorus son of Hagesandros, Hagesandros son of Phania, and Polydoros son of Polydoros." This inscription suggested a clue to the composition, for Pliny had recorded that the Laocoon was fashioned by the three Rhodian artists Hagesandros, Polydoros, and Athenodoros out of a single block of marble. For a little while it was believed that the original Laocoon had once decorated the cave. Tiberius stayed for many years in Rhodes, and he is known to have had a liking for the "full-bloodied" statues by Rhodian sculptors. What more likely than that he should have the original Laocoon brought to Sperlonga?

All over the world the newspapers announced the discovery of the original Laocoon in the cave which served as one of the Emperor's summer palaces. The announcement, however, was premature. Though the colossal snakes and the giant leg fitted into the pattern of Laocoon—the bearded priest and his two sons entangled in the coils of the serpents sent by Apollo—the torsos did not fit. They belonged to full-grown men, not to children. Pliny emphasized that the three sculptors had worked on a single block of marble, but these colossal fragments did not come from a single block of marble. The famous Vatican statue, carefully studied and partially restored by Michelangelo, was also constructed from several pieces cunningly joined together. Nor was there any evidence of a serpent coiling round the giant leg. The theory that the original Laocoon had been found was abandoned. It became increasingly clear that a hitherto unknown composition of several figures had been discovered.

Gradually it came to be realized that the cave had passed through many hands. At various times new groups of statuary had been added, and new grottoes had been carved into the rock. From a Latin epigram dating from the end of the first century it was learned that a certain Faustinus, a rich dilettante and a friend of the poet Martial, claimed to have decorated the cave with a group of statuary commemorating the *crudelitas Scyllae*, "the cruelty of Scylla," the cave-dwelling female monster who wore a girdle of dogs' heads around her loins as she guarded the Straits of Messina. She had six long necks and twelve shapeless legs. Odysseus killed her when he passed through the narrows, but her father cremated her body and she was born anew from the ashes. The archaeologists found a magnificent bearded head crowned with a seaman's cap,

The head of Odysseus from Sperlonga

and they concluded that this might be Odysseus, while the naked torsos might belong to members of his crew.

Yet this theory, though it may well prove to be correct, raises as many problems as it solves. At the right of the entrance to the cave, a ship's prow, still bearing traces of blue, yellow, green, and scarlet mosaic, had been carved in the living rock, and this would be the natural place for Scylla and Odysseus to be joined in conflict. They found the muzzle of a dog and a leg with canine fangs embedded in it nearby. They thought that the problem was solved until they discovered the word ARGO in mosaic on the ship's prow; and though there exist legends of Jason sailing through the Straits of Messina, it was not clear why Jason and his ship should have pride of place at the cave's entrance. Professor Jacopi suggested that ARGO was a generic name used to describe any ship. It is also possible that Tiberius or Faustinus, who lived in the tortured years of Domitian's reign, was solely concerned to elaborate a massive private joke of which the meaning could only be understood by the *cognoscenti.*

While the heap of tumbled statues presented problems which may never be solved, there were enough fine pieces of sculpture to stock a fair-sized museum. The head of Odysseus, with the deep-set eyes and the baroque curls, was a find of the first order, and the figure of the Dardanian prince Ganymede, virtually complete except for a lost right leg, may very well be the statue mentioned by Pliny in his account of the works of the Rhodian sculptor, Leochares, who carved the west façade of the Mausoleum at Halicarnassus. The sculpture represents a beautiful youth caught in an eagle's claws. According to the legend, Zeus took the form of an eagle and lifted him to Mount Olympus, where he was made to serve as cupbearer to the gods. "Leochares portrayed the eagle as a being deeply aware of the treasure it was stealing, and therefore using its talons gently, though the youth's garments protect him." So wrote Pliny, and the description fits the statue perfectly. The heavy waves of the drapery are characteristic of the art of Leochares, who evidently designed the statue so that it could be seen to best advantage from below. The body is executed in Anatolian marble of colors ranging from purple and indigo to sea-green, and the head is of white marble. There seems little doubt that this is a Greek original dating from about 330 B.C. It was probably one of the thousands of sculptures plundered by the Romans from Asia Minor.

Very few representations of Ganymede in sculpture are known. The

The head of Athena from Sperlonga

Vatican has a Ganymede, previously attributed to Leochares, which might serve as an ornament for a Victorian mantlepiece; it entirely lacks the thrust and vigor of the masterpiece found at Sperlonga, and belongs to a time much later than Leochares.

Though the Odysseus and Ganymede are the chief prizes of the excavations in the cave, there were many minor works of great charm and beauty. There was Menelaus with the body of Patroclus, the heads of gods and heroes, a portrait bust which may represent Plato, a smiling Cupid trying on the ferocious mask of a satyr, and two heads of Athena. In one of these she is represented wearing a Corinthian helmet which rides lightly on her curling hair; but as a portrait of the goddess, it is not to be compared with the majestic Athena found the following year beneath a street corner of the harbor city of Piraeus. The sculptor of the Sperlonga Athena simply posed a pretty girl, placed a helmet on her head, and produced a lighthearted version of the goddess.

For many years to come Sperlonga will continue to produce immense fragments of sculpture, like a great womb erupting with monsters. For a period of three hundred years the cave seems to have been an imperial repository for plundered works of art, and there is no knowing what may yet emerge. In winter the sea pours into the cave, and all through the year the spring waters seep through the walls. The sun dances crazily on the foreshore, and the people of Sperlonga, looking down from their cliffs at the sinister mouth of the cave, are still up in arms against the invasion of the archaeologists. The presence of the mysterious and sadistic emperors, Tiberius and Domitian, can still be felt. For another twenty years archaeologists may be exploring the cave, and even then they may be able to solve only a few of the problems that Sperlonga presents.

# TARQUINIA

AERIAL photographs taken over Tarquinia show hundreds of little white pockmarks, as though the whole land were suffering from a raging disease. They cluster in massive groups, spreading over the rolling hills, and seem to be everywhere, though a man walking on the earth sees no sign of the Etruscan graves which are clearly visible from airplanes. Originally all this area was covered with mounds built over stone sepulchers; and when the earth was plowed flat, subtle changes in the chemistry of the soil, due to the presence of the tomb chambers, revealed themselves to anyone looking down from above. The first man to observe these pockmarks was a young Englishman, John Bradford, during flying missions over Italy in World War II. With the aid of his photographs, he was able to pin-point 800 new mounds in Tarquinia alone. By blowing up the photographs he was able to make out the exact shape of each tomb and the position of the entrance.

Others besides Bradford were soon working on the mapping of Etruscan tombs after the war. Carlo Lerici, a distinguished engineer, employed a potentiometer which could accurately distinguish between solid earth and empty subterranean space. He was able to produce graphs

Athletes from Tarquinia

showing the exact position of the hollowed-out tomb chambers. By a further refinement, he went on to invent a special camera called the *sonda fotografica,* a kind of photographic drill, which could be driven through the earth's crust into a tomb chamber to photograph it. In this way he once explored 450 tombs in 120 days. Those who complained about the mechanization of archaeology were reminded that new land reclamation schemes, deep plowing, and the cultivation of fruit trees were quickly changing the face of southern Etruria. The tombs had to be examined quickly, or they would be lost for ever.

On March 26, 1958, there came to light in the southern part of the necropolis of Monterozzi at Tarquinia a tomb chamber with surprisingly vivid paintings in a dramatic style previously unknown. Battles are represented in Etruscan tombs, but they have a curiously stiff quality, the figures like heavy waxwork dolls lumbering onto a stage. These paintings showed an artist responsive to quick movement, living in the second half of the sixth century B.C. The composition is astonishingly human and alive. We see a race between four-horsed chariots, a discobolos about to throw a discus, a foot race won by an old man. Between the discobolos and the runners there is an athlete preparing either to throw himself upon the discobolos or to execute a jump. The athletes are all represented in flesh tints against a brilliant yellow wall. The discus is bright blue, and there are blue and red ribbons along the wall.

Photographs taken by the *sonda fotografica* were immediately developed and transmitted by radio across the Atlantic; and on the following morning they appeared in the New York newspapers. These were photographs of paintings which had not yet been seen by human eyes!

A chariot race from Tarquinia

The head of Bellona from the Cancellaria reliefs

# ROME

THE Palazzo della Cancellaria was built in 1495 for Cardinal Raffaele Riario out of stones quarried from the Colosseum. It is one of the most imposing of the Renaissance palaces in Rome, and for centuries has been the site of the papal chancellery. Today, though it lies outside the Vatican, it is still regarded as a papal enclave, and the Pope is entitled to claim everything found beneath it.

In 1937 the palace was in need of extensive repairs, and to secure the foundations workmen dug deep beneath the building, which stands on the ancient Campus Martius. The workmen expected to find vestiges of Roman ruins, but they were scarcely prepared to find the tomb of one of the closest friends of Julius Caesar—intact, and in an excellent state of preservation. This was the tomb of Aulus Hirtius, who was consul when he fell fighting for Caesar against Mark Antony at the battle of Mutina in 43 B.C. Schoolboys used to know him well, for he was the author of the eighth and last book of Caesar's *Gallic War*. More extraordinary than the discovery of the tomb of Hirtius were the five marble reliefs which were turned inward, facing and partly covering the tomb. Nearby still another relief was discovered, and subsequently a seventh was found under the sidewalk. The first six reliefs came under papal jurisdiction, while the seventh clearly belonged to the city of Rome. Put together, these reliefs formed two monumental friezes showing Emperors being greeted on their return from victorious wars by the attending deities of the Empire. They were not contemporary with Hirtius. They were, in fact, carved over a hundred years later. Whom did they represent? Where had they come from? Had they formed part of a triumphal arch? Had someone deliberately torn them down and flung them into this hole in the earth? Why were they facing the tomb of Hirtius? Was it to preserve them, so that they might be used again?

We shall never know the answers to all the problems raised by the reliefs, but we can make intelligent guesses at some of them. At least one of the figures is a recognizable portrait. Towards the right of the mutilated frieze, we see the characteristic beaked profile of the Emperor Vespasian, the son of an obscure tax collector who rose to the purple because he was an excellent general and his soldiers trusted him. It is a face of considerable power and urgency, and it has been described as having the expression of "a man straining at stool." Behind Vespasian stands a handsome youth holding a cornucopia overflowing with fruit and grapes, representing the abundance brought about by the Emperor. But Vespasian is not looking at the handsome, effeminate youth, who is only lightly sketched into the marble; he is greeting instead another youth whose hair is arranged in elaborate curls, and who is almost certainly his son Domitian. Vespasian places a protective hand on his son's shoulder in the presence of lictors bearing staves, a group of three Vestal Virgins, and a helmeted goddess, who is perhaps Roma, though it is just as possible that she is Bellona, the goddess who presided over the Roman wars. The tall, bearded figure behind Domitian may be Romulus or the Genius of the Roman people. All the figures on the relief are gazing with admiration and approval at the Emperor, who is clearly celebrating his return to Rome after victories overseas. A similar arrangement of figures can be seen on the triumphal arch at Beneventum erected in honor of Trajan.

There are few mysteries about this first mutilated frieze, which clearly represents Vespasian's triumphant return from Jerusalem in A.D. 70. The other frieze is more puzzling. Once again we see an Emperor being greeted by the gods after his victories. Minerva, wearing the characteristic breastplate which shows that she has been modeled after Athena, stands beside the Emperor, while two youthful lictors crowd behind him, and once more we see Roma, or Bellona, in a masterly characterization which derives directly from Periclean Athens. At the center of the frieze stands bearded Jupiter, raising one arm in salute, the other grasping a staff once embellished with a golden eagle. There are soldiers on the right, wearing the uniform of the Praetorian Guard. Gods and mortals mingle as before, but this frieze differs from the other in that the gods are very close to the Emperor and seem to be protecting him. One goddess supports the Emperor's arm with a gesture of exquisite charm. It is as though he were

The relief of Vespasian

The relief of Nerva

so dazzled by the appearance of the gods and goddesses that he needed their support.

But who is this Emperor whose small head is balanced on a neck too thick for it? He is clearly not Vespasian, nor does he wear the thick crown of artificial curls associated with Domitian, the mad Emperor who was hacked to death by his servants. The thickness of the neck, out of all proportion to the "turnip" head, provides a possible clue. As Professor Magi of the Vatican Museum has observed, there are signs that the original head has been reworked, and he suggests that the original head of Domitian has been remodeled to produce an image of Nerva, the mild and unassuming Emperor who was chosen by the Senate in the place of the murdered Domitian. The hair, however, was left unchanged except for the curls on the forehead, which were hacked off. If we look closely at this mysterious head, we can see where the sculptor's chisel has hacked at the hair.

Vespasian and Domitian from the Cancellaria reliefs

If this relief was originally carved in honor of Domitian, it can only have been in celebration of his double triumph over the Chatti and the Dacians in A.D. 83. According to Tacitus, his victory over the Chatti, a north German tribe, was a fraudulent one, and actors wearing yellow wigs took the role of the captives in the triumphal procession. But this double triumph was the only one he celebrated. Domitian was known to possess a special reverence for the goddess Minerva, and her position in the place of honor beside the Emperor is only one more of many indications that he was the Emperor originally represented on the frieze.

We can now attempt to sketch the history of these reliefs: At some time shortly after A.D. 83, Domitian gave orders for the reliefs to be carved, intending them to be used for a triumphal archway, or for the temple he dedicated to Jupiter Custos, or perhaps for the temple he erected in honor of his own family. These were probably completed two years later, and throughout the remaining six years of his reign they were on public display.

With the murder of Domitian in A.D. 91, the reaction set in. Everything that reminded the Roman people and the Senate of the hated Emperor was deliberately defaced; and, like modern dictators who have fallen from grace, he was made to suffer *damnatio memoriae*. The figure of the young Domitian being greeted by the beloved Vespasian was left unchanged. After all, it was not very harmful. The prince was too young to have committed any crimes. But on the second frieze it was decided to substitute the head of Nerva for the head of Domitian. When the frieze was shown to the senatorial committee in charge of public monuments, someone may have observed that a fatal flaw had entered the design. In effect, the entire relief was ruined by the subterfuge, for the new head no longer fitted the body and all the subtle proportions of the frieze were altered beyond repair. Finally the senatorial committee gave orders for the frieze to be abandoned, and accordingly the reliefs were given to the stonecutters who by this time had staked out their shops in the area of the Campus Martius. They placed the reliefs carefully against the tomb of Aulus Hirtius, and there they remained for centuries in the stonecutters' abandoned yard, until the level of Rome rose over them and hid them from sight.

There are many objections to Professor Magi's theory, but it is still the best that has been put forward. Nerva was about sixty-six when he came to the throne, and he had the look of an old man, with sunken cheeks and lined forehead. In the relief he looks remarkably young. Perhaps the chief problem does not lie in the iconography of the frieze, but in the puzzling succession of accidents which have kept it so well preserved. Much of it looks as though it has come straight from the stonecutter's hand.

The city of Rome claimed the slab which was found under the sidewalk of the Corso Vittorio Emanuele and refused to surrender it. Haggling went on for some months. At last the Vatican agreed to surrender a slab of the Ara Pacis in exchange for the missing slab of the Domitian reliefs, and today they stand in a courtyard of the Vatican Museum. In memory of the place where they were found, they are known as the Cancellaria Reliefs.

The head of Nerva
from the Cancellaria reliefs

# SPINA

"SPINA was once a famous Greek city, but it is now only a small village," wrote the geographer Strabo around the time of Christ. "At Delphi you can see the treasury built by the people of Spina, and it is said that they once ruled the sea. They say that in former times Spina lay on the seacoast, but it is now about nine miles inland."

Vase from Spina with Dionysus and Oenopion

Strabo was not alone in celebrating the ancient glory of Spina, once a great city near one of the seven mouths of the River Po. Dionysius of Halicarnassus, who was a contemporary of Strabo, described it even more glowingly. "Of all the inhabitants of the coast of the Ionian Sea they were the most fortunate," he wrote, "for they dominated the sea far and wide and sent the tenth part of the profits of their voyages to the god at Delphi, and these gifts to Apollo were the most splendid of all. Later they abandoned their city, for a horde of neighboring barbarians went to war against them."

So Spina fell, and very little more was heard about the city which may for a short period have been the greatest naval power in the Mediterranean. The temples vanished under the silt from the Po, and they lie there still. But the ancient sleep of Spina is beginning to be disturbed by drainage projects intended to reclaim the estuary of the Po and to transform it into new farmlands. Since 1922 archaeologists, working with the reclamation experts, have been busily uncovering the necropolis of the city. Laboring under enormous difficulties, they were able to unearth almost an entire graveyard containing more than a thousand tombs, finding gold earrings and diadems still lying with the skulls they decorated —skulls which sometimes disintegrated at the touch. They found necklaces of northern amber, perfume bottles from Egypt, and innumerable coins, for every skeleton clutched a few pennies in its right hand as an offering to the god of the underworld. But the most impressive discoveries were the countless Greek black- and red-figured vases, which now have pride

Lion vase from Spina

of place in the museum at Ferrara. These vases come from the very best period of Greek vase making, and they can be dated with considerable accuracy. They begin during the last decades of the sixth century B.C. and end abruptly about the year 390 B.C., when it may be assumed that the city fell before the Gallic invaders.

These tombs provided a complete history of the brief life of the city. The people of Spina seem to have possessed exquisite taste in jewelry; but it was their taste in vases which surprised the archaeologists. One after another, vases painted by great artists emerged from the mud. Many of the painters of individual vases could be identified from existing examples. The ferocious lion, for example, is known to have been painted by an artist called the Berlin Master. The maenad who brandishes her thyrsus as she plucks the beard of the satyr can be identified with an artist called the Goluchov Master. This vase can be dated about 500 B.C. Similarly, the rhyton shaped like a ram's head is known to be the work of the Eretria Master, and can be dated about 430 B.C. The young woman has sent the satyr packing, and that is as it should be. By the same master

Vase from Spina with a maenad and a satyr

is the running girl on an oinochoe, a vase used as a wine jug. It is the same girl, but she is even more charming when she has a whole vase to herself and has space to move in. The double-handled jar by the Altamura Master shows Dionysus with his son Oenopion standing on his knees. Dionysus sits on an ivory chair cushioned by a leopard skin and holds his emblem, the thyrsus, in his left hand. He is all majesty and fatherly devotion, proud of his young son, who wears a crown and flourishes a blossoming tree. Flowers never seen on earth are held by an attendant, and another raises a hand in warning. It is a scene of calm domesticity, but there is a hint of menace in it. The young god will grow up and become a torment to everyone he sets his eyes upon.

Two entire cemeteries have now been uncovered, and more are known to exist. Aerial photographs have revealed the plan of the city laid out on piles in a grid pattern. It is another Venice with another Grand Canal, but the canals follow straight lines. It has been calculated that Spina covered an area of 750 acres, large enough for a population of half a million; and for about a hundred and fifty years the city dominated the Adriatic. Then it seems to have perished overnight, perhaps because it thought itself secure and never troubled to build defense works. Archaeologists have been puzzled to find no weapons in the graves.

Rhyton with Ram's head from Spina

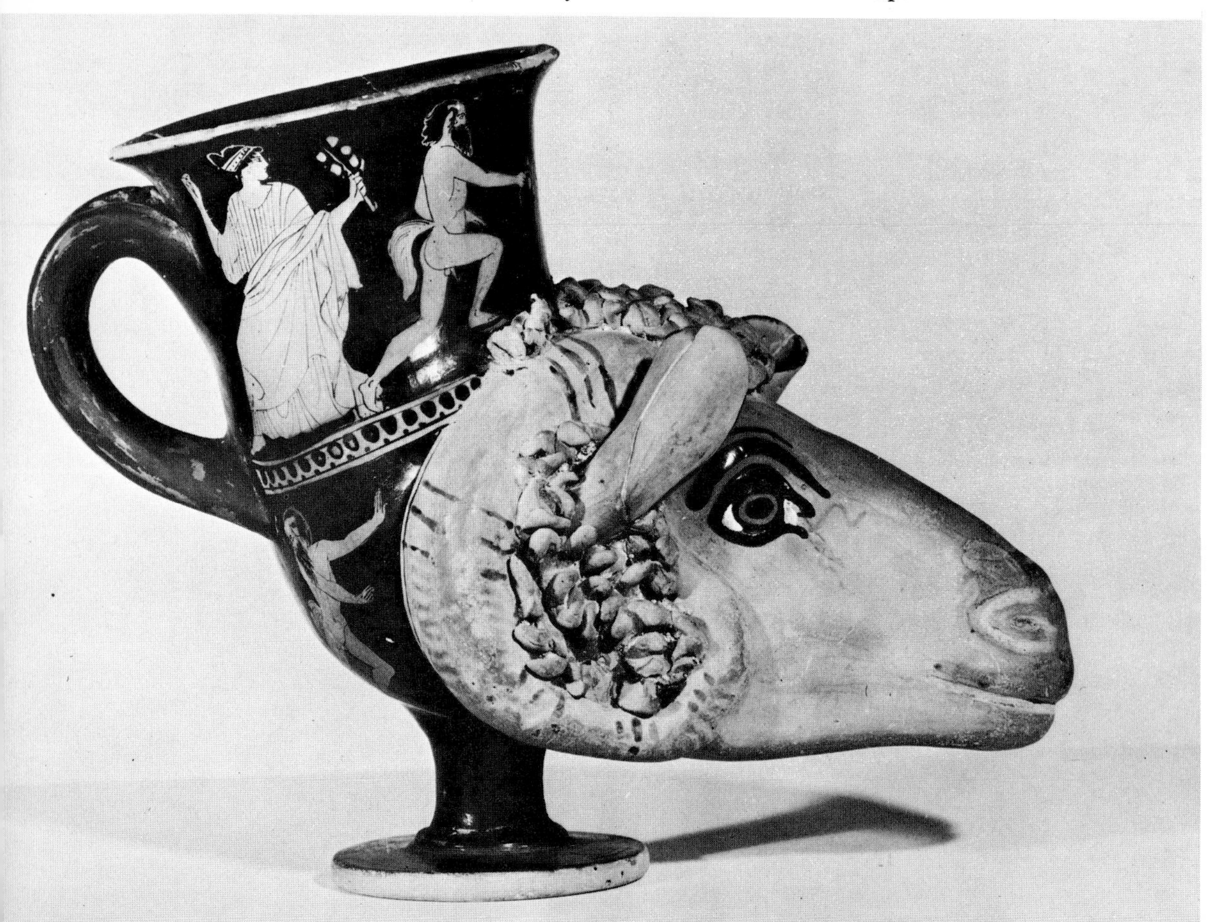

# FOCE DEL SELE

The river Sele, the ancient Silaris, flows into the sea a few miles above Paestum, once the great temple city of Poseidonia. According to the geographer Strabo, when Jason and the Argonauts were coasting along the shores of Italy, they made a landing at the mouth of the Sele and built a sanctuary to the goddess Hera, "the mother of the gods," in honor of their safe landfall. Neither Strabo nor any of the other ancient geographers who casually proclaim the existence of the sanctuary seem to have visited it, and except for the tantalizing information that it was founded by a mythical hero, nothing more was known about it.

Because so little was known, the Heraion at the mouth of the Sele presented a challenge to archaeologists, who have been busily digging along the shores of the river for the last two hundred and fifty years; but at last in April 1934 the sanctuary was uncovered by Dr. Paola Zancani-Montuoro and Dr. Umberto Zanotti-Bianco, two dedicated scholars who carried out their excavations under great difficulties, with only private funds at their disposal. After many years of work and much cutting down of the cork oaks bordering the river, they discovered the foundations of the temple, the altar, and the treasury. They also discovered a mediaeval limekiln, which explained why no walls were left standing. But all these discoveries paled before the far more exciting discovery of some fifty-seven archaic sandstone reliefs and an uncountable number of votive offerings —in one pit alone they found 30,000 terra-cotta images. Suddenly the Heraion seemed to spring to life, and its history over a period of five hundred years as the chief shrine of Hera in Italy could be accurately recorded. Wars, invasions, attacks by pirates, showers of volcanic ash from Vesuvius, all of these had left their mark on the mute stones. In a burst of enthusiasm, Dr. Amedeo Maiuri, the distinguished archaeologist, de-

Metope with two dancing maidens from the Heraion at Foce del Sele

The "leader of the dance" from the Heraion

clared that the excavation of the Heraion was "the most important discovery from a historical, religious and artistic point of view made in Italy during the last fifty years." He was exaggerating, but he had cause for his excitement. The archaic reliefs revealed entirely new and unsuspected aspects of Greek art in Italy.

The most impressive reliefs came from the main temple, and all without exception represented dancers performing a sacred dance, wearing the thinnest of garments and moving with a purely Ionic grace, with grave delicacy and a curious intensity of feeling. Several sculptors' hands can be distinguished, but the same energy seems to flow through all of them. One of these reliefs shows a solitary maiden, her long hair flowing free, looking back at the dancers with an air of authority indicating that she is the leader of the dance: She is evidently a priestess. These sandstone reliefs date from the last quarter of the sixth century B.C., for that particular vigor, those crisp curls and resolute draperies were disappearing by the end of the century. These reliefs must be counted among the masterpieces of Greek art.

Among the votive offerings there was found a small clay statuette of quite unusual beauty, dating from the middle of the fourth century B.C., and representing Hera Eileithyia, the helper of childbirth, naked, on her knees, with two small winged genii at her shoulders, a dove in her right hand. She is giving birth according to the manner of the ancient Greek women. Thus we read in the Homeric *Hymn to Delian Apollo* how Leto "braced her knees against the soft grass" while giving birth to Apollo. The goddess shows no pain nor any anxiety. Quietly, with her head bowed, she awaits the miraculous birth.

Many of these votive offerings showed Hera holding the sacred pomegranate in her uplifted hands. The tradition survived through the centuries, to be adopted by the Christians who in the twelfth century built a church on a spur of nearby Monte Soprana and dedicated it to the Madonna of the Pomegranate. From ancient writers we learn that votive boats filled with flowers were offered to the goddess, and today the pilgrims who climb the mountain paths to the church carry votive boats filled with flowers and wax candles.

Terra-cotta statuette of Hera Eileithyia from Foce del Sele

Boy with ostrich from the Corridor of the Great Hunting Scene at Piazza Armerina

# PIAZZA ARMERINA

TO honor the two thousandth anniversary of the birth of Augustus Caesar in 63 B.C., Mussolini decided to place special funds in the hands of archaeologists working on projects which would "illustrate the imperial traditions of the fatherland." Among the projects chosen was a ruined villa in central Sicily three miles from the small cathedral town of Piazza Armerina, where excavations begun as far back as 1889 had revealed the existence of important mosaics. These early excavations brought to light a vast mosaic representing Hercules battling with the giants, which showed that artists of quite extraordinary skill had been at work in the villa. Between 1937 and 1939 a few more mosaics were found, including a lively vintage scene and a brilliantly colored and sumptuous picture of African animals being herded onto waiting ships, presumably to be exhibited in the Roman arenas. Then the war came, and the excavations came to an end.

The mosaics of the Piazza Armerina might have been completely forgotten had it not been for an astute archaeologist who was able to catch the ear of the Prime Minister. The archaeologist pointed out that if more mosaics were found—and he suspected that acres of them lay just below the surface of the earth—visitors would come flocking to central Sicily to the benefit of the Italian tourist trade. Accordingly, large grants were made, and in the years immediately after the war the archaeologists went to work in earnest. What they found exceeded all expectations. The villa proved to be an immense rambling palace, built in a style which was completely unknown and unsuspected, wandering over four hills and floored with mosaics stretching over an area of 3,500 square yards. At least thirty million *tesserae* had gone into the making of these mosaic floors.

Who built the palace, and what exactly it was doing there in central Sicily on the western slope of Monte Mangone, are questions which are still being debated by scholars. No one knows the names of the artists who made these brilliantly colored floors, or where they came from. There are only the rarest references to the palace in historical times, and of these the most definite is an obscure phrase in a letter of St. Gregory the Great. It was quite clearly an imperial palace, for none but an Emperor could have afforded to build it, but there exist no imperial rescripts announcing that great matters of state were discussed there or that armies set out from its gates. If the palace had been swallowed up in an earthquake, no one would have lamented the loss. Yet this palace must have rivaled Nero's Golden House, which has vanished, or Diocletian's palace at Spalato on the Dalmatian coast, which still survives.

Anyone coming fresh to the scene is dazzled by the sheer vastness of the place. Room opens into room: an endless series of private chambers and porticoes and courtyards, nearly all of them provided with mosaic floors. Many columns and a few walls are still standing, but the main effect is of an amazingly complex series of buildings of which the entire superstructure has been blown away in a tempest, leaving only a brilliantly colored floor plan and a few vestiges of ruins. What remains of the palace sits in a valley, shut in on all sides by hills thickly covered with pines, cypresses, oak trees, and hazel shrubs. There is nothing majestic about the site—no grand view, no dominating position. A stream winds nearby, and an aqueduct once brought fresh water to the palace. In ancient times the hills were more thickly wooded, and they were filled with game. Accordingly, it has been assumed that the palace was built on the site of a favorite hunting lodge.

When the archaeologists went to work after the war, they quickly discovered they were dealing with shapes and contours which had no comparable forms in classical times. There were buildings shaped like clover leaves, horseshoes, flattened eggs, parallelograms. The axes were staggered, and no effort had been made to maintain a general design. Gradually it came to be realized that the architect was a master craftsman, who by abandoning formal design had permitted life to flow freely through the buildings. The wild, wandering ground plan was no more irrational than the curling and twisting of the tendrils of vines; and the palace must have been a joy to walk about in.

Though today we miss the contrasts of straight and curving walls, and the sudden leapings of columns, the palace is still a joy to walk through. The marble *tesserae* glitter in the Sicilian sun, and if you are prepared to pay an extra fee, a guardian will swab them lightly with oil. Then the richness of the coloring, the blazing orange, yellows, and greens, seem to rise palpably off the ground and fill the air around you. There are also acres of mosaics in Monreale Cathedral near Palermo, but these are arranged in carefully worked ribbons along the walls. There is not that effect of immediacy, of things happening and rising under your feet, which is characteristic of Piazza Armerina.

The Emperor Maximianus attended by guards from the Corridor of the Great Hunting Scene at Piazza Armerina

When the mosaics were uncovered, scholars set to work to discover the original owner of the palace from clues in the individual portraits, in the clothes worn by the huntsmen, in the themes of the mosaics. One of the most obvious clues was the low, cylindrical skullcap worn by the principal figures and known to be characteristic of the age of Constantine. Another clue was the ivy leaf, sacred to Hercules, in the shoulder badge of one of the guards attending a man who is evidently an important dignitary. Hercules himself appears on so many of the mosaics that it may be reasonably assumed that the owner held Hercules in high honor. There is a picture of the Circus Maximus in Rome with only one obelisk standing. This must have been the obelisk erected by Augustus, for after A.D. 357 it was known that a second obelisk was erected by the Emperor Constantius II. Here and there we come upon a young prince with a round face, a crooked nose, and a pronounced squint. So we may conclude that the palace belonged to an Emperor living shortly before A.D. 357, who had a special devotion for Hercules, and whose son squinted. Such an Emperor did in fact exist. He was Maximianus Herculius, a Pannonian soldier who was raised to the purple by Diocletian in A.D. 285 to become co-ruler of the empire. He was described by the Byzantine author Ioannes Malalas as "of good height, vigorous, straight hair half-white, with perfect beard, dark complexion, strong nose, fluent in speech." This description corresponds well enough with the brutal and troubled Emperor who is seen sipping from a wineglass, closely attended by two guards with flaming red shields. The thick beard, the strong nose, the "half-white" hair coming straight down over his forehead provide an inescapable portrait of a man who has thrust his way to power from lowly origins. Ioannes Malalas adds the information that his son Maxentius squinted.

Here and there we find other portraits. In the small hunting scene there is a man with a long, triangular face offering incense at a wayside shrine to Diana. He seems to be preparing an outdoor barbecue, but is in fact offering burned incense from a *patera* which he holds in his left hand. There is no doubt that he is a royal personage, for he wears a purple, gold-embroidered tunic. From the bulbous forehead, straight hair, tilted eyebrows, and small chin we recognize him as the Emperor Constantius Chlorus, "the pale one," who was one of the two Caesars appointed by Maximianus and Diocletian when they abdicated in A.D. 305. The young prince standing behind him and holding a sorrel horse by a

Constantine and Constantius Chlorous from the Small Hunting Scene at Piazza Armerina

halter is evidently his son Constantine, who eventually wrested the Empire from Maxentius and became Constantine the Great.

Portraits abound in the hunting scenes, each face seen sharply and individually, even though the bodies are often wooden. Towards the shrine of Diana come two huntsmen with a wild boar trussed on a carrying pole, while a hound barks below. These faces are instinct with life, and we would recognize them if they entered the room. The wide-eyed boy and the sallow-faced man lean forward under the weight of their burden, but the sense of movement, the excitement of the chase, seems to come chiefly from the faces with their deep awareness of what is happening around them. The face of the boy with his arm flung round an ostrich is deliberately framed between the tail feathers and the ostrich's swanlike head, and there is nothing in the least fortuitous about the arrangement. We see an officer of the court pushing a wheeled cage. There is no energy in his hands or legs, but there is more than enough energy in his face and in the robust folds of his tasseled gown. Without being able to draw a good human figure, the artist has succeeded in conveying human strength by concentrating on the features and on whatever elements of life can be adduced from the clothes.

The artist is at his best when he depicts animals. Then he lets loose with controlled vigor and a deep affection. The two lumbering oxen, dragging the wheeled cage, are evidently based on quick sketches, though the mosaicists must have worked hundreds of hours and employed thousands of marble chips to transfer the sketches onto the marble floor. Three deer are being driven into a net. These deer are not imagined: They have been seen hurtling into nets and falling exactly as the artist sketched them rapidly on his sketch pad. A more studied composition shows a bare-kneed huntsman who has been gored by a wild boar and lies bleeding at the base of a tree, having thrown down his spear. He is saved from yet another attack by the huntsman who stands behind him, his long spear aimed at the boar's heart. The boar is wading through a stream, shaggy and wet and weary of the baying of the hounds. The master stroke comes with the hound's head—that strange head which seems to have emerged from the roots of the tree, a head without a body. The hound shows all its teeth as it hurls defiance at the boar, scenting the death that will come soon. The scene has a passionate, instinctual life, and the ferocity we associate with Assyrian reliefs.

Deer herded into a net

Boar hunting scene from Piazza Armerina

We can see how well the artist designed the mosaic if we take a closer view of the fallen huntsman. The ripe, rounded bole of the tree is like some swelling fruit; the stippled lines moving in all directions on the tunic give life and movement to an otherwise ill-drawn body; and once more we see a face full of life and awareness, balanced by the hound's head, which is deliberately sharp-angled, not rounded in any way. The artist who originally drew the scene had watched a wild boar dying at his feet.

But the supreme artistic achievement at Piazza Armerina lies with the designer of the great mosaic of the labors of Hercules. Furious speed and ferocious energy are at the command of the artist. He distorts, twists, tilts these creatures of his imagination until he has shaped them into strange, almost abstract patterns of power. In one scene we see the gray bull of Marathon about to charge, while the Lernean Hydra, with the face of a woman and the body of a snake and with little snakelets dangling from her hair, hovers above the bull's head. Above both of these monsters, one of the man-eating horses of Diomedes is about to destroy its rider. This

Detail from mosaic in the Hall of the Labors of Hercules

horse of Diomedes shows a mastery of abstract form which has no equal in art until our own day. Enormous power surges from those fantastic beasts which can never have been observed from nature. They are the product of a nightmarish intensity of vision. Hercules himself, his labors over, is depicted by the same artist with extraordinary power in a scene which shows him crowned with laurel leaves and wearing the shirt of Nessus, which will soon bring about his death in agony. In that heroic face there is something of the brooding energy we find many hundreds of years later in the Byzantine mosaics of God in majesty.

Only a few of the mosaics at Piazza Armerina have this richness of texture and unrestricted energy. Many are derivative, and some are lifeless. The charming love scene set in a small cubicle is completely preserved, but it is more notable for the complexity of the ornamental design than for the central medallion. The more famous "Bikini girls" probably represent dancers of an aquacade receiving their prizes—the blue *tesserae* on which they stand representing water. The poet Martial speaks of actresses dressed as Nereids swimming in the Colosseum at Rome, and

"Bikini girls" from the Hall of the Ten Maidens

these halters and bathing slips may very well represent the costumes of Nereids. It is just possible that the scene represents a beauty contest. Altogether ten "Bikini girls" are shown, all of them equally wooden, dating from a period considerably later than the other mosaics.

Maximianus Herculius did not enjoy his palace for long. When his son Maxentius seized Rome and proclaimed himself Emperor in A.D. 306, he fled from Sicily and took refuge in Gaul with Constantine, who had married his daughter Fausta. There for years he lived peacefully, until it became evident that he was in secret correspondence with his son. Constantine taxed him with the crime, and in A.D. 310, at the age of sixty, Maximianus committed suicide.

Gibbon described him with summary judgment. "Ignorant of letters, careless of laws, the rusticity of his appearance and manners still betrayed in the most elevated fortune the meanness of his extraction. War was the only art which he professed." It was not true. He protected and encouraged artists, and he will be remembered as the man who built the greatest palace in all of Sicily.

Medallion of lovers from Piazza Armerina

Acroterium representing Victory from the Stoa of Zeus Eleutherios

# ATHENS

THE Agora or market place was the heart of Athens. There, on a broad space below the Acropolis the Athenians set up their booths, shading them from the sun with awnings, and built temples, and managed their affairs, crowding and jostling one another. Sacred processions wound their way through the Agora. More and more temples went up, more statues, more government offices, until in time there was hardly room to move among the innumerable buildings scattered over those forty acres at the base of the Acropolis. Here were the law courts, the war office, the civic centers, the library, the bureau of standards, and the state archives, this last housed in a small building attached to the Temple to the Mother of the Gods. Here was the mint; and here, too, was the *bouleuterion* or parliament, where the five hundred elected officials who controlled the destiny of Athens had their meeting place and refectory. Athenaeus, a scholar of the late second century A.D., gave a list of things which might be found in the Agora: "Figs, witnesses, grapes, turnips, pears, apples, men waiting to give testimony, medlars, porridge, honeycombs, chickpeas, lawsuits, beestings, beesting-puddings, myrtle, allotment-machines, irises, waterclocks, laws, indictments." It was only a partial list. There were conjurors and sword swallowers, jewelers, cloth merchants, bankers, cattlemen, philosophers, and many more. The entire economy of Athens, earthly and divine, passed through the Agora.

In the morning the noise of the Agora was deafening, and loudest of all were the fishmongers who cursed their customers and freshened rotten fish so that it looked like new. The market police were kept busy seeing that the fair-trade laws were obeyed, and running after thieves and rascals of all kinds. There was so much noise that sometimes the lawyers and the city councilors could not make themselves heard, and then orders would be given to rope off large sections of the Agora near the law courts and the parliament house. Then for a while the haggling and the shouting would die down, but there would be uproar again the next morning.

For the Greeks, trade, government, and worship were never completely separated, and it seemed perfectly appropriate to them that the Agora should combine the functions of a market place, a civic center, a complex of temples, and a shrine for the heroic dead whose monuments were scattered about the busy streets. Kings and conquerors raised monuments to themselves. The great Cimon raised memorials in honor of his victory over the Persians, and planted poplars and willows. Wealthy men also endowed buildings, or put up statues, or refurnished the temples. About 150 B.C. Attalus II, king of Pergamum, built the famous stoa which bears his name as a gesture of affection for the city where he had studied as a youth. Augustus raised a temple to himself, and Agrippa, his chief minister, built a great theater called the Agrippeion. By the middle of the third century A.D. the Agora was crowded with statues and altars and ornate temples and civic buildings in gleaming marble; some were seven hundred years old and others were new. The life of Athens still poured through the brilliantly colored market place, but time was running out.

The reconstructed Stoa of Attalus in the Agora

In A.D. 257 Athens was savagely attacked by a barbarian tribe from the north—the Herulians, about whom very little is known. This sudden surprise attack led to the destruction of most of the buildings in the Agora, though the Temple of Hephaestus was left unharmed. The Herulians went on to destroy more Greek cities, while the Athenians took what measures they could to defend themselves in the future. Realizing that they could no longer defend the great outer wall, they decided to build a wall through the Agora with the rubble left from the invasion. The Agrippeion had gone up in flames, but the scorched stones could still be used. Broken statues were thrown into the defense works. Everything that could possibly be of use in building a wall, even small terra-cotta statues, was hammered into place. The rear wall of the Stoa of Attalus became a part of the new fortifications. Of the Agora itself, nothing remained.

Today, seventeen hundred years later, the Agora is coming to life again, thanks to the munificent donations of John D. Rockefeller, Jr., who has largely financed the work of the American School in Athens. The market place has been excavated to its foundations and the Stoa of Attalus has been restored to all its original beauty. In 1931, when the work was begun, nearly the whole of the area was covered with houses. These were bought and demolished. Then began the exhausting task of removing twenty-eight acres of topsoil before the ground level of late antiquity could be reached. About 300,000 tons of earth were removed before the ancient bones of the law courts and some twenty other immense buildings could be seen once more.

The main purpose of the archaeologists was to make a study in historical depth of the ancient buildings which once stood in the Agora. By examining foundations and employing all the resources of archaeological detective work, they were able to make a time plan of all the temples and altars and public buildings in the area they had uncovered. They came to know which building stood in what place at what time, and very often they were able to trace the existence of successive buildings on the same site. Only a part of the wall of the Stoa of Attalus remained; but they were able to calculate the building's exact shape and set it up again exactly as it was when King Attalus offered it to the city. They learned the exact height of the columns, the shape and color of the terra-cotta roof tiles, the design of the shops which fronted on the marble colonnade, and how the doors opened and closed. They found sockets in the wall which gave them the height of the original roof beams, and traces of marble-chip flooring gave them a clue to the original floors. With the aid of a multitude of similar clues, John Travlos, the architect of the school's excavations, accomplished something never attempted before. He restored an ancient classical monument to its original perfection, though only a few bricks remained.

This "second" Stoa of Attalus was completed in 1956, and immediately became a museum housing the antiquities discovered during the excavations.

The discoveries made by the American School of Classical Studies ranged over immense distances of time—from neolithic pit graves to late Byzantine icons. They found no great bronze figures of the gods like the magnificent works discovered at sea off Cape Artemision and in the soil of Piraeus, but they found thousands of household objects, so that it is now possible to reconstruct the habits and customs of the Athenians with a greater degree of accuracy than ever before. And sometimes they found objects of singular beauty.

The most beautiful of all was a winged Victory, one of the acroteria of the Stoa of Zeus Eleutherios. The wings, the arms, and part of the head have vanished, but even so she gives a sense of abundant and majestic life. Full-breasted, with heavy limbs, she yet comes lightly to earth, her draperies flowing like waves around her, and no one could ever mistake her for an earthly visitor. Her thin chiton has slipped down from her left shoulder, clearly revealing the modeling of her neck and shoulder and the grace of the head turned back, it seems, for a last look at heaven before she comes to live among mortals. The archaeologists believe that she was made between 421 and 415 B.C., in the brief flowering between the Peace of Nicias and the disastrous Sicilian expedition.

The kneeling boy tying a fillet round his head, with a vase mouth rising out of his elaborately curled hair, belongs to an earlier age. He has the characteristic bulging eyes, heavy chin, and half-smile of the archaic period, and he can be roughly dated around 530 B.C. Though cracked wide open, with half his back destroyed, he was found in excellent condition and the pieces could easily be put together. This terra-cotta boy, found in the rubble at the bottom of a thirty-foot-deep well, was probably an oil flask, the kneeling position being adopted to enable him to sit solidly on a shelf. Kneeling statues are very rare among the Greeks, though common in the Saite period in Egypt (660–525 B.C.), and it may be assumed that some Egyptian influence is at work. There are traces of red

Terra-cotta boy tying a fillet from the Agora

paint on the hair and lips, and the enormous eyes are painted jet black. The ribbon is a modern addition, but fits so exactly into the scheme of the design that it has become essential to it. The enormous toes, the hands raised in an attitude of surrender, the anatomically impossible chest, and the vase mouth rising out of his head like the funnel of a steam engine, are all very odd indeed. But the details fuse into a remarkably vivid whole. It is one of the most appealing terra cottas ever found.

Egyptian influence appears again in the powerful portrait of a priest found in 1933 in the very early stages of the excavations. That heavy, brooding face is earnest with defiant sanctity. His head is shaven and he wears a rolled fillet with a star at the center, which perhaps indicates a high rank in the priestly hierarchy. The features are Egyptian, and accordingly the portrait presents problems of dating and provenance. It may be a Roman work of the Republican period.

Portrait head of a priest from the Agora

The portrait of the Julio-Claudian prince can be dated more accurately to the first century A.D. This, too, was found in 1933 in the rubble of the fortification wall. It has been claimed that it represents Augustus Caesar and was carved at the time of his visit to Greece in 21 B.C. Is it a heroic portrait of Augustus, with just sufficient likeness to be nearly convincing? The beauty of Augustus approached femininity, but there is nothing feminine here. It is a masterly representation of a prince of the Julio-Claudian line, but no one knows for certain who he is.

Portrait bust of a Julio-Claudian prince

The head of the youthful goddess with her hair swept in the high curls familiar from the portraits of the Antonines was found in a well at the northwest foot of the Areopagus. Like the Julio-Claudian prince, she is highly polished and in an excellent state of preservation. The face is severe, imperious, the harshness of the nose and mouth softened by the rounded cheeks. The broken lower lip gives her the odd expression of someone suddenly coming to an abrupt stop in the middle of a sentence. The heavy lids suggest moodiness, a calm despair.

There is nothing moody or despairing in the marble head of Hercules, discovered, like the youthful goddess, during the excavations of 1947. Hercules wears the lion skin, but he is himself a lion, licking his chops. The back of the head is unworked, suggesting that it once formed part of a marble relief. A comparison with a rather similar head of Hercules on one of the metopes of the Athenian treasury at Delphi shows this to be an even greater work of art. It is about half life-size, and can be dated about 520 B.C.

Marble head of Hercules from the Agora

This Hercules with the robust curls and bulging eyes is not smiling: He is meditating murder, solemnly contemplating his own divine powers of destruction, yearning after his own magnificence. One should beware of the sleepy smiles of archaic sculptures. These gods are only too determined and wide-awake. Paint him as he was once painted, with golden lion skin, straw-colored beard, blue eyes, pink cheeks, and blood-red mouth, and he becomes more formidable. The head is only six inches high, but there is a ferocious power in him.

The sleeping child would seem to be a Roman copy of a Hellenistic work. Strangely, the ornate curls and the heavy ribbon do not detract from the impression of pure and simple charm, of overwhelming ease. The child is drowned in sleep. The legs are broken at the knees and one arm is missing, but, as so often happens, the essential elements have been preserved. We scarcely notice the amputations, and if we notice them, we hardly care. There are some roughnesses which can be ascribed to the Roman copyist. One suspects that the Hellenistic original was a masterpiece.

Sleeping child, Roman copy of a Hellenistic work

The Stoa of Attalus has been completed, but the work of the American School of Classical Studies at Athens goes on. A good part of the Agora is still buried. The Stoa Poikile and the library of Hadrian remain to be excavated when funds are available and when the Greek government gives permission to tear down the houses standing on the sites. These excavations are usually slow and arduous work, prohibitively expensive, and not overly exciting. Then suddenly a sleeping child, a head of Hercules, or a winged Victory emerges; and the sun seems to dance in the sky.

Head of a youthful goddess from the Agora

# PIRAEUS: THE MARBLE RELIEFS

ABOUT the year 448 B.C. the sculptor Phidias began work on the monumental chryselephantine statue of Athena Parthenos, which was solemnly dedicated ten years later. Nearly forty feet high, and made entirely of gold and ivory except for the supporting framework, Athena stood in splendid isolation amid the half-darkness of her temple on the Acropolis. She wore a towering helmet bristling with plumes, and on her breast lay the fearsome aegis with the Gorgon head, the symbol of her divine power. In her right hand stood a winged Victory six feet high, while her left hand supported a shield and a spear. Her shield and sandals, and her high pedestal, were richly covered with reliefs. Everything about the statue was sumptuous, noble, powerful, and a little frightening. She was more than a maiden goddess, for she represented the fierce and unrelenting energies of the city.

In time the ivory of Athena's arms and face, and the gold of her robes and shield, were broken up or melted to fill a barbarian treasure chest. She vanished, leaving behind only some small and unimpressive replicas, which hardly convey the imperious beauty of the original. The relief on the outer surface of the shield, representing the battle between the Greeks and the Amazons, was famous. From fragmentary Roman copies we are enabled to glimpse some of the details of that wild battlefield. A relief known as the "Strangford Shield," now in the British Museum, shows the Greeks furiously slaughtering the Amazons, stabbing them, stoning them to death, treading them underfoot, and hurling them off walls. Though the Roman shield is evidently only a copy of a copy, at a vast remove from the original, it preserves the movement and excitement of the battle.

Until 1930 the Strangford Shield and some small fragments in the Vatican and in the Museo Nuovo in Rome were the only known representations of the shield carved by Phidias.

In the winter of 1930 dredging operations were being carried out in the main basin of the harbor at Piraeus. The buckets of the dredgers hit upon some slabs of marble, and divers were sent down to explore the sea bed, where they found the remains of a flat-bottomed transport, which had evidently burned and sunk while lying at anchor. Most of the marble reliefs had no artistic merit. They were designed for the export market, and were probably intended to decorate Roman palaces during the second century A.D. But two of the reliefs immediately caught the eyes of the experts, for quite unexpectedly they shed light on the shield of Phidias.

The marble relief of the falling Amazon

The Strangford Shield shows an Amazon falling over a cliff and pulling an armed Greek down with her. This same scene is depicted on one of the reliefs which was raised out of the sea-slime in Piraeus harbor, with the difference that the new relief gives the impression of being a reasonably close copy of an original. The Piraeus reliefs showed one Greek and one Amazon within a rectangular frame. Evidently the design on the shield had been cut up into small squares and minor changes were made so that a copy of the famous frieze of the battle of the Amazons could be set up on the walls of some Roman house. The figures are exactly the size we would expect if they had been copied directly from the shield of Phidias.

The relief of the Amazon throwing herself off the cliff and pulling her adversary with her to destruction is an extraordinary achievement. There is no parallel in Greek art to the boldness of this design, with its dramatic use of large areas of empty space to set off the violence of the encounter. Complex rhythms flow back and forth between the figures. The Greek pulls at the Amazon's hair; she grips his wrist. It is certain that he will fall with her, for the heavy shield gives her momentum—the momentum of despair. The battle-ax which has slipped out of her hands is not spinning in mid-air, but caught in an instantaneous moment of time in a position which suggests that it is momentarily at rest, waiting for her to follow. The study of the hovering Amazon owes much to the type of the Victories, who are usually seen descending to earth and still hovering as they lightly touch the ground.

The Strangford Shield

Another relief shows a helmeted Amazon running up a rocky slope to attack a warrior in a heavy cloak. She, too, appears on the Strangford Shield. It is possible that she is Hippolyta, Queen of the Amazons, confronting Theseus, Prince of the Athenians. Here again there is a sense of crackling energy, of an event which will be decided in a moment of time; but the cool, controlled energy of the former scene is lacking.

The marble relief of the attacking Amazon

Plutarch tells a curious story about the punishment which came to Phidias for representing himself on the shield: "For he showed the likeness of himself as a bald old man holding up a stone with both hands, and he also made an excellent likeness of Pericles battling an Amazon, his spear-holding hand flung in front of his face in a way which cleverly concealed it if you looked from the front, though the image was clear enough if you looked from the sides. For this crime Phidias was imprisoned, and he died of a disease in prison, or, as some say, he was poisoned by the enemies of Pericles."

Somewhere in the harbor at Piraeus there may be other reliefs of those scenes which appear in miniature on the Strangford Shield. There Phidias is shown hurling a rock at an Amazon who has fallen at his feet, and even less gallantly, Pericles is stomping an Amazon to death and at the same time transfixing her with a spear. These are recognizable portraits, but sketchy. One would give a great deal to see them as they were on the shield of Phidias.

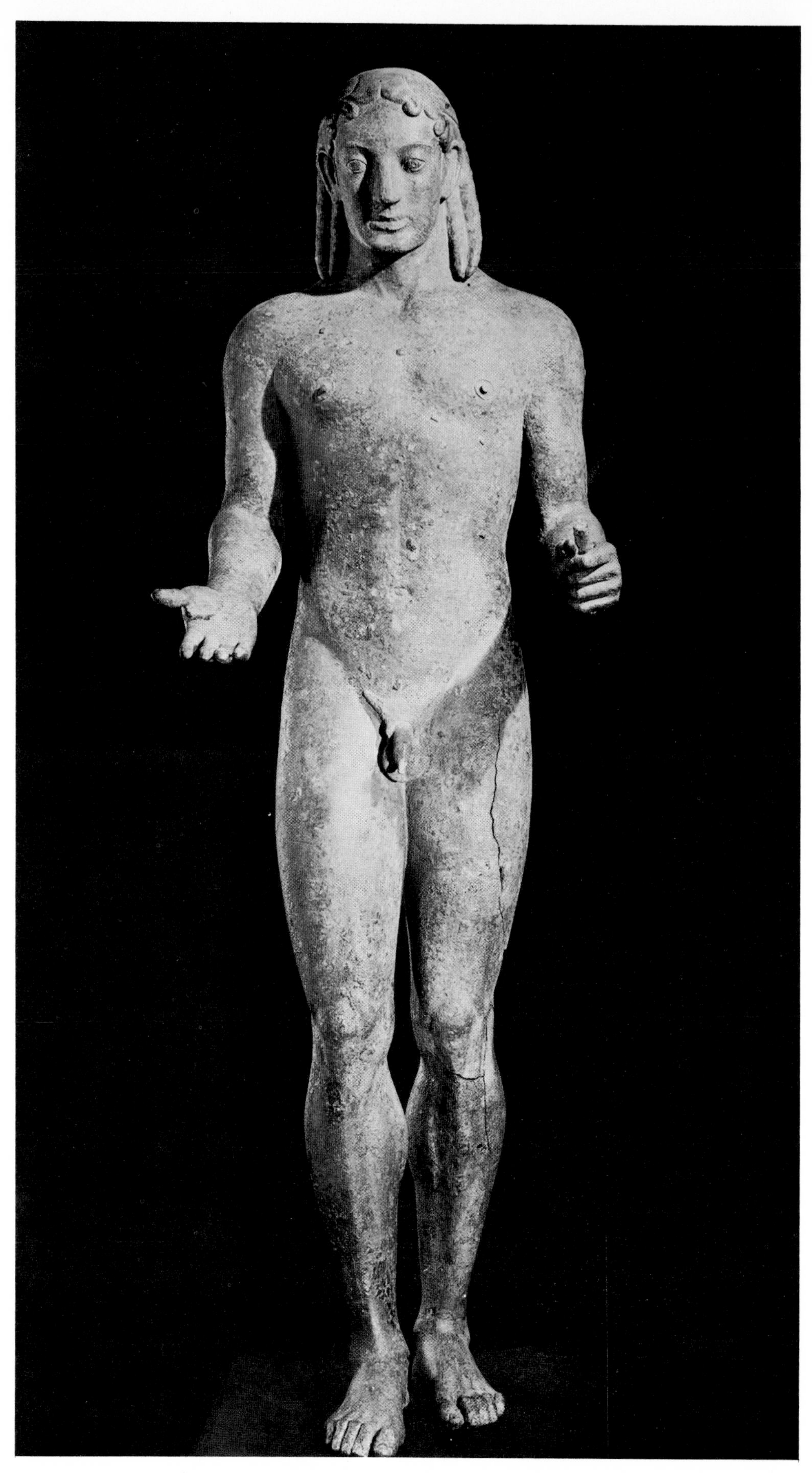

The bronze Apollo from Piraeus

# PIRAEUS: THE STATUES

ON July 18, 1959, two workmen pulling up the pavement to repair sewers in a busy section of Piraeus, saw a finger protruding from the earth. It was a very hot day, and at first they scarcely believed what they saw. Then they realized that it was a bronze finger, and they ran to the works supervisor with the news. He ordered all work to be stopped and telephoned Demetrios Kalandonis, the director of the Piraeus Archaeological Museum, who came running to the scene. Soon from all over Piraeus and Athens people came running to see the statues which were being unearthed at the corner of Filonas and King George I streets. The two workmen, Andreas Sakellion and Nikos Kordonoris, had unwittingly been standing on the greatest hoard of Greek statues found in this century.

All through the morning and early afternoon the work of uncovering the statues went on in the intense heat, to the mounting excitement of the crowd. First, the two hands of a bronze youth were uncovered. Even before the rest of the statue was excavated, it was evident that this was Apollo, for the left hand was closed and had once held a bow, while the right hand was open in the characteristic Apollonian gesture. Then it was seen that the left arm was blackened as though by fire; and mingled with the earth covering the statue were ashes, cinders, charcoal, and fragments of roof tiles. So from the very beginning it was possible to guess that the statue had been in a repository which had burned, and that after the roof caved in the statue had been abandoned and forgotten.

Between the arms of the Apollo there was found a white marble herm of a familiar kind, for many copies of it are known. This was Hermes at his most august, ringleted, with a curling beard, looking more like a Persian emperor than a Greek god. It was carved, according to the inscriptions which can be seen on many of the surviving copies, by Alcam-

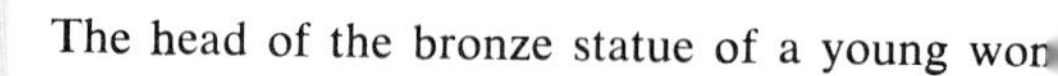
The head of the bronze statue of a young wom

enes, the pupil of Phidias, that same Alcamenes who produced the marvelous and still surviving figures on the west pediment of the temple of Zeus at Olympia.

A little later a second bronze statue was found, this time of a young woman with curled hair and heavy draperies, remarkable for the delicate modeling of the features. The head of the young Apollo had been lying against her legs, and like the Apollo, she was slightly larger than life. One of her arms was missing, but she was otherwise in a fine state of preservation, and her eyes, made of semiprecious jewels, were still in place. Apollo could be dated roughly to the last quarter of the sixth century B.C., but this young woman clearly belonged to a later epoch. She is believed to be a creation of the Hellenistic period, probably the second half of the fourth century B.C.

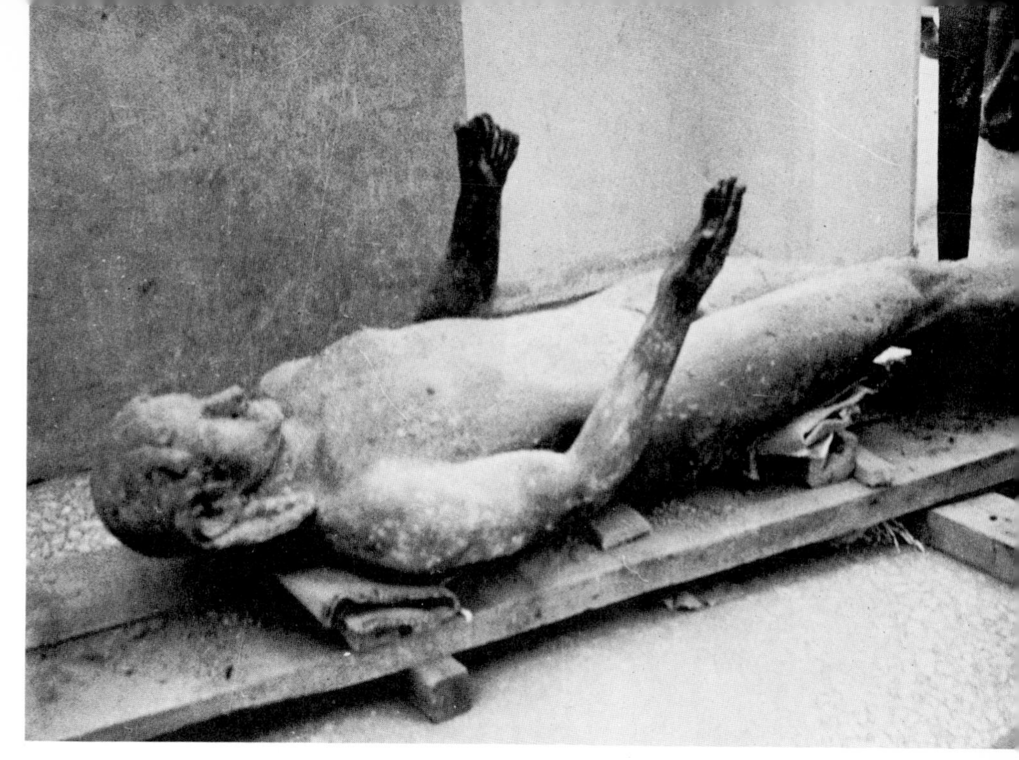

The bronze Apollo shortly after discovery

By five o'clock on that burning July afternoon the two bronze statues and the marble Hermes were disengaged from the earth and carefully lifted into a truck. They were then taken to the Piraeus Archaeological Museum—the truck moving at a walking pace so as not to damage these heirlooms from the past which had been so miraculously preserved—and half the population of Piraeus followed the truck in a kind of processional triumph.

The archaeologists were convinced that they had accidentally come upon a hoard of treasure, and that many more statues must be buried nearby. All through the following days work went on, but it was not until July 25, exactly a week after the first discovery, that more statues came to light. In quick succession they found another herm, a companion to the one already found, a huge bronze statue of Athena wearing a helmet, a bronze Artemis carrying a sheaf of arrows, and a bronze tragedy mask, a replica of a mask worn by a tragic actor, which probably ornamented some ancient theater in Athens. The jewel of the collection was the Athena, who was clearly Hellenistic and seemed to have been made by the same artist who fashioned the bronze maiden lying beside Apollo. Her helmet bore representations of owls and griffins with spread wings, and there was the magic aegis embroidered with snakes upon her breast. Her eyes were of semiprecious stones, which still glittered. One arm was flung out, and she may have once held a small Victory in her hand, and the other hand may have rested on a shield; but of the Victory and the shield there was no trace. She was seven and a half feet high, majestic but not imperious. There was something tentative, gentle, and sweet-tempered in her expression, and she could never have been made when Athens was at the height of its power. Yet she had the eagerness of youth, and it was not difficult to imagine her half-open lips summoning men to war.

Nothing like the helmeted Athena had ever been found before. Her appearance was of course known from coins, from small bronzes, and from the crude marble statue in the National Museum at Athens, which is believed to be a miniature replica of the chryselephantine statue made by Phidias for the Parthenon. But none of these possesses the gentle heroic grace of the Athena of Piraeus.

The great bronze statue of Athena from Pir

How did these statues happen to be buried at a busy street corner in Piraeus? The archaeologists soon found themselves in possession of a reasonably complete explanation. The clue was a small bronze coin found among the statues, bearing representations of Athena wearing a Corinthian helmet and Zeus holding the lightning, with the letters ΑΘΕ, meaning "of the Athenians," together with a star between two half-moons, which was the symbol of Mithridates the Great. The coin could be dated accurately to the year 87–86 B.C. It happened that in March of 86 B.C. the Roman dictator Sulla fulfilled his long-standing ambition to destroy the power of Athens and to kill as many Athenians as possible. At midnight he brought his army up to an undefended gate, broke through, and slaughtered everything in his path. The area of Cerameicus flowed with blood. "There was no counting the number of the dead," wrote Plutarch, "and to this day we can only guess at the number by the amount of ground covered with blood, while those who fell to the sword were no less than those who took their own lives out of sorrow for the city which was being destroyed." Plutarch adds that shortly afterwards Sulla went on to Piraeus "and burned most of it." The flame-marks on the left arm of the young Apollo may well have come from that burning.

Having destroyed Athens and Piraeus, Sulla went on to Asia Minor where he fought a series of campaigns against Mithridates; and when he had concluded a treaty of peace with Mithridates, he returned to Athens to collect a vast store of booty, including the entire library of the philosopher Appelicon of Teos which contained all the surviving manuscripts of Aristotle, and set sail for Italy with twelve hundred ships. On these ships were all the statues he could lay his hands on; but his lieutenants overlooked the statues which lay under blackened roof beams in Piraeus. The marble reliefs found in the harbor of Piraeus may have been lost at the same period, for the sunken ship also bore traces of fire.

Sulla despoiled Athens of all her treasure. Caravans of statues were taken to Rome, where they survived until the barbarian invasions. Athenian bronzes have rarely been found in the soil of Attica. Four or five bronzes of major importance have been reclaimed from the sea, but with the exception of the Charioteer of Delphi hardly a single bronze of the classical period has been reclaimed from the Greek earth. The bronze Apollo is the earliest full-size representation of the god in existence, being earlier by more than a quarter of a century than the great Apollo of

Bronze Tragedy mask

Piombino in the Louvre, which was found in Tuscany in the small seaport which was the port of embarcation for the island of Elba.

The Apollo of Piraeus still wears an archaic smile, and belongs to a time long before the Persian invasions. He has that curious mingling of stiffness and lightness which has come to be associated with the sculptures from the pediment of the temple of Aphaia at Aegina, but he was already old when that temple was young. When found he seemed to have a light down on his cheeks, the result of the "tubercular disease" which attacks impure bronze, and there were the same downy bubbles scattered over the body. This down could be melted away by putting him into a bath of distilled water, but a more serious problem was presented by the clay which lay beneath the bronze skin, for the statue was made by the *cire perdu* process by which molten bronze is poured between two layers of clay separated by wax. The clay beneath the bronze had expanded, and here and there had forced its way through the bronze. Very delicately and carefully the clay had to be extracted. In several places the experts working on the clay found the fingerprints of the original sculptor. Gradually the corrosive salts and incrustations on the statue were washed or chipped away, and from being a strange mottled chalky white mingled with light green, it came to assume the deep sea-green color of the Charioteer of Delphi. Then, and only then, was an invisible solution of metal lacquer shot deep into the pores of the metal, to seal it from climatic changes. As it stands now in the National Museum at Athens, so it should be in a thousand years time.

The two marble herms needed little treatment. They suffered from none of the diseases which sometimes attack ancient marble. The Artemis, the bronze maiden found with Apollo, and the great Athena all needed the treatment given to Apollo. It will take time, for the process of cleaning and preserving them is an expensive one, and there are only a few experts capable of undertaking the task. When the work of restoration is completed the statues will all be exhibited at the National Museum in Athens for a few months before being returned to Piraeus. The people of Piraeus have made it quite plain that they will go to war with Athens unless the sculptures are returned to them.

Marble Herm from Piraeus

# MYCENAE

ON November 28, 1876, Heinrich Schliemann sent a telegram to King George of Greece, announcing that he had unearthed "immense treasures from ancient times, all in pure gold," together with the tomb of Agamemnon. Only three years before he had found another hoard of gold in the walls of ancient Troy, and it pleased him to think he had discovered the imperial regalia which had once decorated the heads of the Trojan kings and queens.

Schliemann's discovery of the grave circle at Mycenae took place in the presence of Greek scholars and in the full light of publicity; his Trojan discoveries were more mysterious affairs, so mysterious indeed that even today we are not sure exactly where or how they were unearthed. With the discovery of the grave circle at Mycenae, Schliemann, the most unscientific of archaeologists, heralded the modern science of archaeology.

Excavations continued at Mycenae at intervals during the following years without any great success, but although small objects were recovered, there was a general impression that Schliemann had uncovered all the treasure that was to be found there. Seventy-five years later, in the spring of 1951, Greek archaeologists working on the restoration of the so-called Tomb of Clytemnestra outside the citadel found three carved stones jutting out of the ground. They reminded the archaeologists of the stone markers around the grave circle discovered by Schliemann, and it was thought that another grave circle might be found there. They started digging, and in the course of the next two years twenty-four graves were found within the circle. Daggers with ivory pommels, engraved gems, gold ornaments, a crystal bowl, a gold mask, and many gold ribbons were found, together with innumerable lesser treasures. Evidently

Gold and ivory sword hilt from Mycenae

a whole dynasty had been buried here. Who were they? Why were they buried outside the citadel? Did they rule before or after the dead kings found by Schliemann? Not surprisingly, the discovery of the second grave circle raised as many problems as the first.

When Pausanias visited Mycenae about A.D. 150, he learned of a tradition that Agamemnon was buried inside the citadel, while Aegisthus and Clytemnestra were buried beyond the walls "because they were thought unworthy of being buried within." This tradition must have been more than fifteen hundred years old even in the time of Pausanias. Eighteen hundred years after Pausanias wrote, it has been partially verified. Pausanias heard that there were two graveyards, and two have been found. So do traditions live through the centuries.

The names of the kings buried in the grave circles remain unknown, and though we are reasonably sure that Agamemnon and Aegisthus are not among them, even that tradition must be treated with a lingering respect.

The amethyst portrait gem

Among the jewels found in the new excavations was a tiny amethyst gem less than a centimeter in diameter, engraved with a vivid portrait. It is a singularly powerful face, and may very well reproduce the features of a king. His hair is combed over the forehead, and the back hair falls heavily to the shoulders in the manner of the long-haired Achaeans. The enormous deep-set eyes, the long, straight nose (with both nostrils indicated), the high cheekbones, the large ears, the beard brushed forward, all these combine to form a recognizable portrait. We imagine such a man as heavily built, and in fact the skeletons in the graves were unusually large, some of the men being six feet tall. Could this be Aegisthus, the murderer of Agamemnon?

A strange gold mask with forbidding features was also found. No one can even guess whom it portrays, or indeed whether it was a man, woman, or child. The precise purpose of such masks is still unknown. All have the telltale small holes beside the ears which suggest that they covered the dead face and were kept in place by a ribbon fastened behind the head. What appears to be a heavy beard is perhaps only a covering for the chin and throat.

Gold mask from Mycenae

In a nearby grave there was a sword, with gold sheathing and an ivory pommel which had partly flaked away. The gold sheathing bore the restless scroll patterns familiar from previous discoveries in Mycenae and Crete, but the shoulders of the grip were quite unusual, with the heads of mythological animals with lozenge-shaped eyes carved on them. There are two pairs of these strange heads; and though they evidently relate to the power within the sword, and vaguely resemble dolphins, goats, bulls, and lions, no names can be given to these beasts. They probably arose out of the fantasy of the artist and may never be identified.

The magnificent crystal bowl in the form of a duck may have come originally from Egypt. Found in fragments, it was perhaps the greatest single artistic find within the second grave circle. The duck's head is gracefully bent back to form the handle, while the tail forms the spout. It is very small, scarcely more than five inches long, but completely satisfying. Elegance, wit, and beauty, exquisite workmanship, and superb mastery over a difficult medium are all present. This crystal duck was a fit companion for the young princess in the tomb.

Crystal bowl in the form of a duck

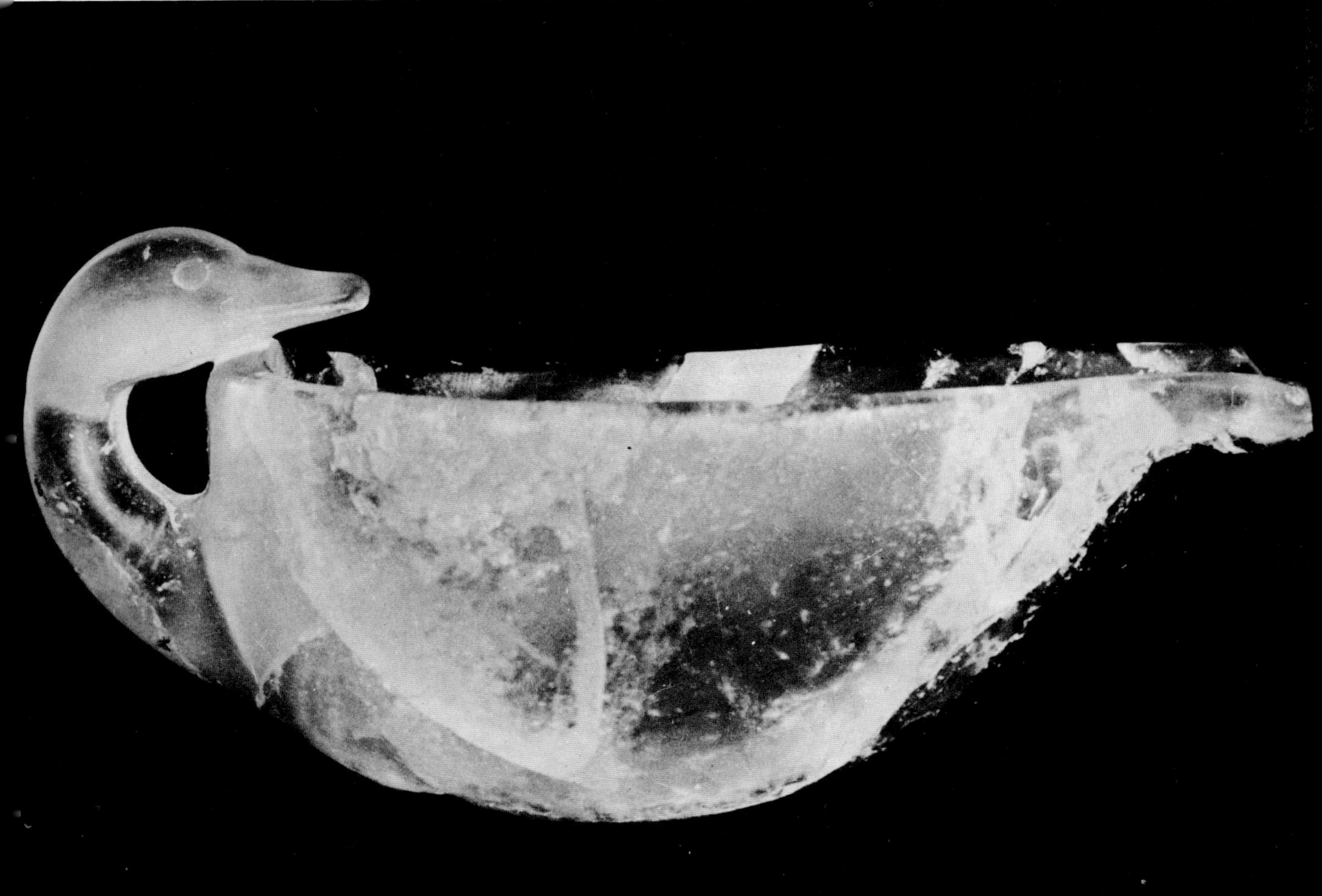

# VRAVRON

FOR a long time it has been known that the small town of Vravron on the Attic coast twenty-four miles from Athens was the site of the ancient temple of Artemis Vravronia (or Brauronia). Here young girls, usually between five and ten years old, were presented to the goddess Artemis, the chaste sister of Apollo, and entrusted to her care. At these festivals the girls were clad in saffron-colored garments, and some wore bearskins, and the "dance of the bears" took place around her altar. Here, too, according to one of the legends, came Iphigenia and Orestes after their escape from Tauris, building the temple as a thank offering for their safe return to Attica. Artemis Vravronia was so important that a precinct was dedicated to her on the Acropolis itself.

Votive relief with gods and goddesses from Vravron

Since 1946 Greek archaeologists have been working to uncover the temple which lay buried below the level of the fields. It was particularly arduous work, for water continually rose and had to be pumped out, and the archaeologists spent a good deal of time floundering in the mud. They found the temple and a prehistoric cave, believed to be the site of Iphigenia's tomb. The temple was built in the Doric style, sixty feet long and thirty feet wide; and the cave, too, took the form of a sanctuary, and was almost as large. A great number of votive offerings, clay statuettes, and pieces of pottery were found in the swampy soil. In *Iphigenia in Tauris* Euripides refers to the strange sacrifices and rituals which took place in the temple. Once every year, to celebrate the safe arrival of Orestes, a priest drew blood from the neck of a man; and to commemorate the death of Iphigenia, the jewels and garments of women who died in childbirth were offered to Artemis. Inventories listing the ornaments and garments of these women were found within the temple.

Among the votive offerings were two fine reliefs, both small, executed in a monumental fashion. On one relief, only three feet long, we see the gods gazing with an air of expectancy towards some awaited guests. We do not know for certain who the gods are, though it is likely enough that the three on the left are Poseidon, Artemis, and Apollo, who appear together in a similar grouping on the east frieze of the Parthenon. Poseidon's right arm is raised, and he seems to be beckoning to his guests, but in fact he is merely supporting a trident which would have been painted onto the relief. Artemis, too, is leaning on a now invisible staff. In his broken right hand Apollo may have been holding the sacred *patera.* His robes fall in simple folds to the ground, and he stands there quietly, unlike the young woman on his left whose robes swirl around her. She is evidently a messenger of the gods, a wingless Victory. The hooves of a horse can be seen behind her, and she is leading this horse into the presence of the gods. Behind the horse there was probably a chariot containing Iphigenia and Orestes—but all this is mystery, for the relief is broken off just at the point where it might reveal its secret.

The sculptor of this relief was an authentic master; and in the treatment of the figures and draperies he is the equal of the sculptor of the Parthenon frieze.

The other relief is a lesser work, dating from about the middle of the fourth century B.C. We see a whole family moving into the presence of the towering figure of Artemis, armed with her bow and with one of her hounds standing upon her altar, the sacred *patera* lying in her right hand. She stands there as she must have stood in the temple, elegant and serene, while the worshipers pay their quiet tribute. The aged have the place of honor, as they always do among the Greeks. One woman carries a child in her arms. A boy places a protective hand on the horn of a bull which will soon be sacrificed, and children stare into space, wondering what all the fuss is about. At the very end of the procession a woman enters, carrying on her head a basket of offerings for the goddess. An inscription reads: "Dedicated in prayer to Artemis by Aristonikê, wife of Antiphatis of Thoroi."

It is a simple thing with no pretensions to great art, but rarely has the piety of an ordinary Greek family been expressed so vividly. There are altogether seventeen figures on this relief, which is little more than three feet long. They come silently, with undemonstrative pride, into the presence of the goddess, and there is about them a charm not easily forgotten.

Votive relief of a family bringing offerings to Artemis

# PELLA

ABOUT the end of the Peloponnesian war, King Archelaos decided to move from the remote and beautiful fortress of Aigai and build himself a palace at Pella, near the uncertain frontier of the river Axios." So wrote Thucydides towards the end of his history, telling us nearly all we know about the foundation of the city where Alexander the Great was born and Euripides died.

Pella was built on the slope of a hill, and defended by impenetrable swamps. It must have been a very small and desolate place until some fifty years after its foundation when Philip II became the conqueror of Greece as the result of a series of lightning attacks on undefended territories. From this obscure hill-fortress orders went out to all Greece; in another generation Alexander the Great was sending out orders from Pella to the entire world.

Little was known about Pella until the spring of 1957 when excavators discovered two column drums from the palace, and later uncovered the foundation walls. This palace proved to be the largest ever unearthed in Macedonia, containing brilliant pebble mosaics dating from the time of Alexander. The mosaics are evidently based on contemporary paintings, the long, low composition of "The Lion Hunt" being a suitable decoration for the wall of a portico, with its use of a deep blue background and splashes of glittering gold to relieve the pale whiteness of flesh. An idealized figure of Alexander stands at the right; his curved sword is raised above his head, and his flaring cape, imitating wings, is filled with colored shadows of pale blue, ocher, and gray. Here and there the artist has inserted thin strips of bronze to suggest outlines, a technique rarely encountered in later mosaics. These bronze wires outline an arm, the profile of a face, the details of the lion's mane, and their effect is continually pleasing.

The "Lion Hunt" mosaic

The lion is a *tour de force*, being charged with the energy of creation, and at the same time maintaining a kind of emblematic remoteness. The mane is a blaze of gold, and so is the lion's mouth, while the rippling muscles are patterned in blue and bronze. The far leg is shadowed, but very sketchily, and there are almost no shadows on the white bodies of the two young heroes. Perhaps the artist, like the ancient Chinese, felt that the human body should be seen in the full light of the sun, unshadowed. The blue river pebbles have the effect of making the sky shimmer with starlight.

"The Lion Hunt," though the best, is only one of many mosaics found at Pella. We see a griffin attacking a stag, and a naked Dionysus riding on a panther. Dionysus has the soft flesh of a woman, but the head is severely masculine, and even the crown of ivy leaves cannot reduce his masculinity. These mosaics point to the astonishing elegance of this palace which only a hundred years before had been a hill-fortress on the edge of a swamp.

Idealized figure of Alexander from the "Lion Hunt" mosaic at Pella

Detail from the pebble mosaic at Vergina

# VERGINA

WITHIN sight of Pella, in the foothills of the mountains of Pieria, there stand the ruins of another Macedonian palace, which has come to be known as "the Palace of Vergina" after a small village in the neighborhood. The existence of this palace has been known since 1885 when a French archaeologist began to excavate it. He opened up the eastern section of the ruins, but a small church on the site prevented any further exploration. What he found was sufficiently impressive to suggest that he had discovered the palace of the ancient Macedonian city of Valla. He thought the palace was built in the fifth century B.C., but modern Greek archaeologists believe it was built in the first quarter of the third century B.C., probably by Antigonus Gonatas, the grandson of one of Alexander the Great's generals, who proclaimed himself King of Macedonia in 283 B.C.

The palace was forgotten for over fifty years. Then in the spring of 1938 Professor Romaios of the University of Thessalonica began work on the site. In one season, from March to October, he was able to make a survey of the whole palace, uncovering large areas to the south and west, but excavations were discontinued for lack of funds. They were resumed in 1954, and two years later Professor Romaios uncovered the magnificent mosaic floor of an audience chamber in the southern wing of the palace.

Like the mosaics in Pella, these are constructed of thousands of river pebbles. But where in Pella the designs represent heroes in combat with lions or the gods at play, these floors show a pronounced feeling for abstract design. Within a meandering border we see a flower exploding into a pattern of intricate tendrils, as sumptuous as any Persian carpet.

The original has been cracked by earthquakes and is difficult to photograph; but the schematic drawing which we reproduce shows the richness of the design.

Among the glories of this pebbled carpet are the four feminine forms emerging at the four corners. They are half plants, half women. Full-breasted, well-fleshed, wearing pearly crowns, earrings, and close-fitting garments, these women have a calm majesty of their own. There is a sumptuousness in these designs and flowering women which is very rare in Greek art, and indeed some Oriental influence is clearly at work.

The design of the pebble mosaic at Vergina

# CORINTH

WHEN the traveler Pausanias visited Corinth about A.D. 175, he found a flourishing city. There was the gleaming temple of Aphrodite on the summit of the golden mountain, more temples on the slopes, and the city itself with its market places, theaters, temples, and sanctuaries lay spread out around the base of the mountain. Sculptures from the classical age were standing, and in one of the temples he came upon an image of Hercules said to have been carved by the legendary sculptor Daedalus. Just outside the city walls he came upon a burnt-out temple to Apollo, but such ominous glimpses of a violent past were rare. Everything about the city gave an impression of permanence, as though it had been there forever.

When Pausanias visited it, Corinth was actually little more than two hundred years old. The ancient Corinth, richest city in Greece, founder of innumerable colonies, and leader of the Achaean League, vanished in 146 B.C. when the Roman consul Lucius Mummius ordered it razed to the ground, having previously taken the precaution of loading everything of value, including a whole forest of great statues, onto his ships. For a hundred years after that Corinth was an uninhabited wasteland until Julius Caesar took pity on the desert of tumbled stones and ordered it rebuilt under the name of Laus Julia Corinthiensis. The first settlers were a group of freedmen who prospered by digging up the tombs of the ancient Corinthians and looting them, selling the bronzes and vases on the Roman market.

Corinth survived, but there can be few cities which have suffered so many disasters. The savage Herulians crossed the isthmus in A.D. 267, but were beaten off. An earthquake shattered the city in A.D. 375, and what was left was burned to the ground by Alaric the Goth in A.D. 395. There was another great earthquake in A.D. 521. The Normans sacked the city in the twelfth century; the Crusaders captured it in the thirteenth; a Florentine prince took possession of it in the fourteenth; and it came under the rule of the Byzantines shortly before the Byzantine Empire perished at the hands of the Turks. It was leveled to the ground in an earthquake in 1858, and there have been further earthquakes, notably in 1928 and 1930, to remind the Corinthians of the impermanence of their city. Today, reduced to the size of a village, Corinth still looks out on the blue waters of the isthmus, living on its memories.

The ruins remain—acres upon acres of them, reaching from the sea to the great rock citadel of Acrocorinth with its crumbling Byzantine fortress. Seven massive archaic pillars of the temple of Apollo remain, having survived for twenty-five centuries. Great paved roads, market places, shrines, temples, and colonnades can be traced out; but wandering among the ruins of Corinth to anyone except a trained archaeologist is rather like climbing among boulders on the seashore. The tenfold ruin of Corinth is complete.

Since 1896 the American School of Classical Studies at Athens has been attempting to bring order to this chaos. The greater part of the city wall has been traced, and the sites of most of the temples have been cleared. Pausanias describes with great care the celebrated fountain of Peirene, begun by the tyrant Periander and completed by the millionaire Herodes Atticus. There were once ornamented grottoes, marble floors, archways, and an open-air fountain. At first the archaeologists were unable to find any trace of it. They were pondering the problem when one of the younger members of the staff decided to explore the garden well of the house where the archaeologists were living. He climbed down into the well and at the bottom found himself in running water. He followed the dark passageway until it widened, saw portions of two archways rising in front of him, and remembered Pausanias' description of "the chambers made like grottoes where the water flows into an open-air fountain." He had found the fountain of Peirene in his own garden.

For nearly seventy years the American archaeologists have continued to make discoveries. Perhaps the loveliest of all is the small terra-cotta dancer of the fourth century B.C. found recently in the sanctuary of Demeter on Acrocorinth. In that sanctuary, according to Pausanias, were

Marble head of a young woman from Corinth

Terra-cotta dancing girl from Acrocorinth

"images that are not exposed to view." Those images have vanished, but the small terra-cotta offerings brought by worshipers have been found in profusion.

The statue of Augustus, slightly over life-size, was found almost intact, with traces of paint still showing on the eyes, lips, and hair. The deep red color on the hair once served as an undercoat for gilding. Augustus wears the veil over his head, indicating that he is fulfilling his priestly office as Pontifex Maximus. He is in deep thought, with an expression of severity rarely to be seen in his portraits. It is evidently an official portrait, and it must have stood in a prominent position in the Julian Basilica. The subtle modeling of the features goes beyond the usual commissioned statues of the time.

The head of the marble statue of Augustus

Something of that same brooding quality is seen in the head of Fortuna, the guardian goddess of the city, with her heavy battlemented crown riding on two waves of curls, as though riding on the sea. She belongs to the end of the first century A.D., but in the modeling of the lips and chin she is closely related to the Augustus. Care weighs heavily upon her, and her crown oppresses her. One imagines she would be glad to toss it away.

Head of the guardian goddess of the city of Corinth

The winsome young woman with the curls cascading over her forehead belongs to the same period, and came perhaps from the same workshop. Her features are vulgar—her nose too wide, her upper lip too small—and she can never have been truly beautiful; but she has a charming impudence and grace. She is a country girl lost in dreams, with more life in her than the Fortuna or Augustus ever possessed. The holes in her curls may have supported a floral crown.

The mosaics from a Roman villa just outside the city walls are among the most prized possessions of the museum at Corinth. These mosaics are more controlled, more classical in feeling, than those of Piazza Armerina. There is an astonishing delicacy and strength in the Dionysus

Herdsman mosaic from a Roman villa in Corinth

of the central medallion. Tamed by the Romans, he is all fire, but will not rage. So it is with the herdsman leaning against a tree and playing on his pipe, while the goats ruminate and the cattle graze. He glows with color, but he prefers the contemplative life, forgetting the wars and disasters which were visited on Corinth for centuries.

The modern traveler, wandering through the ruins of Corinth—the city which Cicero called *lumen totius Graeciae*, the light of all Greece—finds himself sharing the preoccupations of the herdsman. Rome has her ruins; Corinth has only her ruins of ruins. No casual visitor to Corinth would guess at the immense power this city once possessed, and how magnificently it was embellished by beneficent tyrants and emperors. All that remains are the seven columns of the Temple of Apollo set in a wilderness and the fragments set in the museum. In the end the herdsmen has the last word.

Mosaic medallion of Dionysus from Corinth

# SAMOTHRACE

THIS island with the savage hills lies in the northeastern Aegean, guarding the sea lanes to the Dardanelles. Here in 1863 the French consul in Adrianople discovered in the ruined Sanctuary of the Great Gods a broken statue of white Parian marble, which had once decorated a monumental fountain. This was the Winged Victory of Samothrace, headless, armless, and with only one unbroken wing. The statue was removed to the Louvre, but many years passed before it became generally recognized that France had taken possession of a prodigious masterpiece. Some twenty-six years later the consul returned to Samothrace and removed the gray marble ship's prow which had once borne the Victory.

Even today no one knows what sea battle was commemorated by the Victory, and scholars are still disputing over naval victories which took place in 306, 258, and 190 B.C. Nor does anyone know how she held her arms or what she was holding in her hands, though the discovery of her right hand in 1950 suggests that she was holding nothing at all. It would appear that her arm was extended in a gesture of greeting.

We associate Samothrace with the Victory; but the ancient Greeks associated the island with the religion of the Great Gods and a mystery cult involving a sacred marriage (*hieros gamos*) and a dramatic initiation into the secret rites of the Great Mother and her attendant divinities. There is considerable mystery about the cult. The rites were especially favored by sailors, who during the initiation ceremonies received purple scarves to protect them on the high seas.

Herodotus was initiated into the cult, and the royal house of Macedon owed a special allegiance to it. It was said that Philip of Macedon first met Olympias, a princess of Epirus, while attending the rites. She became his queen and the mother of Alexander the Great. Thereafter each successive ruler of Macedon seems to have offered gifts to the sanctuary. When Ptolemy II Philadelphus, captured the island in the early third century B.C., he offered two handsome buildings to the sanctuary in his own name and in that of his queen, Arsinoe II. Under the Romans, pilgrims in large numbers continued to visit the island, but little is known about its history in later antiquity. Defenseless and outflanked, the mysteries abolished by order of Theodosius the Great, the island sank into gradual decay.

In October 1444, Cyriacus of Ancona, a merchant-diplomat with a profound interest in ancient Greece, visited the island and copied inscriptions in the town and in the sanctuary, but little more was heard about the island until the discovery of the Victory of Samothrace in 1863. French and Austrian archaeologists worked briefly on the site in the sixties and seventies of the last century, and finally in 1938 New York University undertook a full exploration and excavation of the great sanctuary. Nearly all our present knowledge of the sanctuary and of the mystery cult derives from the work of Dr. Karl Lehmann and his assistants.

The frieze of the dancing maidens from Samothrace

The most exciting discovery took place in 1949, when they unearthed a graceful frieze of dancing maidens. Some fragments of the frieze were already known, but this new fragment was in a finer state of preservation than any discovered previously. Musicians accompany the dancers, and they clasp hands lightly, and gaze at one another with expressions of calm delight. The relief evidently describes a ritual dance. There is evidence to show that it must have been carved about 340 B.C., but the dancers are deliberately represented in an archaic style, apparently in allusion to the venerable nature of the rites. The figures are only a few inches high, but they possess a monumental grandeur.

In the same year another Victory of Samothrace was found by Phyllis Williams Lehmann. The figure is life-size, carved in Thasian marble, and seems to have fallen from its place on the roof of the hieron in an earthquake about A.D. 200. The broken pieces were found buried carefully beside the building. When the fragments were put together, the Victory was seen to be an unusually slim-waisted maiden, headless, with huge wings, and with only one arm. An odd spike emerging from her right shoulder once supported her wrist, for originally she was pouring a libation into a *patera* held in her left hand. The spike would have been invisible when the statue stood on the roof of the temple.

The new Victory improves on acquaintance. There is a charm and delicacy in the modeling of the torso, and the too-heavy folds of the cloak wrapped round the lower part of her body give dramatic emphasis to her youthfulness. The Victory in the Louvre possesses a godlike vigor: She could walk over the waters, still the tempests, and destroy any ships in her path. The Victory in the museum at Samothrace is a young maiden who would run to shelter at the first sign of a storm. She is like a young girl who has wrapped her mother's gown around her knees, and admires herself in a mirror. She is vulnerable, and there is nothing in the least divine about her; but she is all the more welcome because she belongs to the ordinary world of Greece.

Marble Victory from Samothrace

Corinthian helmet from Olympia

As far back as 1500 B.C. there were temples to the gods in the fertile valley of the Alpheos in the western Peloponnese. These were temples to gods who were later dethroned—to the Great Mother and Kronos and Pelops, the local hero who gave the Peloponnese its name. About 1000 B.C. Olympia became associated with Zeus, "lord of the heavens and all the spaces of the earth," who had the appearance of a brooding, middle-aged man of vast authority and dignity. In his honor were held the games which were to continue at Olympia until nearly A.D. 400. History, as the Greeks knew it, began in 776 B.C., when for the first time the names of the winners were officially recorded.

The Olympic Games were held every four years, but the worship of Zeus was continuous and all through the year men came to pay homage to him in his temple. At first the temple was cumbrous and crude, made of mud brick, but with the victory of the Greeks over the Persians a new temple was offered to him in the belief that he had played a decisive part in the liberation of Greece from foreign bondage. Within the temple stood the colossal gold and ivory statue of Zeus by Phidias, "a statue of such majesty," wrote Quintilian, "that it was equal to the god." Other temples to the lesser gods were built in the shadow of Zeus's shrine, statues were erected to the heroes and the winners of the games, and soon the Olympian sanctuary was crowded with gifts from all the nations and colonies of Greece. Not even the sanctuary of Apollo at Delphi was as sumptuous.

The worship of Zeus survived the coming of the Christian Emperors, lasting until A.D. 394 when Theodosius the Great issued an imperial rescript abolishing the games and the worship of the pagan god. Ironically, the last recorded victor in the games was a Persian boxer from Armenia.

In A.D. 426 the Emperor Theodosius II decreed the destruction of all pagan temples within his empire, and the temple of Zeus became a church. Then in the days of Justinian a series of great earthquakes brought ruin to Olympia. The huge columns were flung outward, and some pieces of the pediment were later found thirty feet away. In time the site became a swamp, and malaria made it uninhabitable, while floods covered it over with silt and debris from the neighboring hills. Even its name perished, and in the sixteenth century it was known as Andilalo, a wretched little village which no one ever visited.

It was a German, Johann Joachim Winckelmann, who identified the site at last in 1768, but he was unable to realize his dream of uncovering the ruins, for he was murdered in Trieste in that very year. The French made some tentative excavations in 1829, uncovering one of the metopes, which is now in the Louvre. Later Heinrich Schliemann employed all his resources, which were considerable, in order to obtain the right to dig from the Greek government, but it was the German Academy of Science with the Crown Prince Frederick as the moving spirit which eventually took on the excavations. Dr. Ernst Curtius, the historian and archaeologist, was placed in charge of the project, which involved the removal of an entire village and twenty feet of clay and silt before the foundations of the temples could be uncovered. The German archaeologists were rewarded with the discovery of nearly all the marble statues of the east and west pediments of the temple, and nearly all the metopes. They found the Hermes of Praxiteles. Between 1876 and 1882 they cleared most of the temple area and opened up an entirely new chapter in Greek art. The discovery of the beautiful and commanding figure of Apollo from the west pediment would alone have made the work worth-while.

The Germans have continued to work at Olympia ever since. The spectacular finds of Dr. Curtius have never been surpassed, and it is unlikely that they will be, but every year brings its new increment of knowledge. The complete plan of the temple area is now known, and the history of Olympia for a thousand years can be fully documented. Especially important are the Corinthian helmets and embossed shield bands found recently. The shields themselves have perished, but the bands show scenes from mythology which seem to be copied from sixth-century reliefs. Helmets and shields presumably hung as offerings in the temple of Zeus.

These helmets were works of art. Some were found in almost pristine condition; others have derived an added grandeur from the abrasions of time. The Corinthian helmet, illustrated here, is studded with nails and outlined above the eyes with a peculiarly delicate meander. Among the other helmets found by the Germans was a very strangely shaped one with a dedication crudely scratched along the rim, reading: "To the god, from the Athenians who took it from the Persians."

Often on these votive offerings the name of the god is omitted, for since the offerings hung in his temple there was no reason to name him. The bronze runner, four inches tall, has the words "I belong to Zeus" inscribed on his right thigh. Found in Olympia, he is clearly of Attic workmanship and dates from about 500 B.C. There is still some archaic stiffness in him, but he is standing on the verge of a new epoch when severity will give way to more fluid contours. There is a companion piece by the same artist, showing the boy standing upright, in the National Museum in Athens.

The boy leans forward, waiting for the word of command to begin the race. He is all muscle and controlled energy, the outflung arms tensed and ready, the features singularly calm. Only the hair, elaborately curled, suggests the passionate love of self-adornment among the young Athenians of the time.

We see those heavy curls again in the terra-cotta portrait of a young woman, which still bears traces of the original paint. She is a little later, and may be dated about 490 B.C., the year of the battle of Marathon.

Bronze runner from Olympia

Terra-cotta head of a young goddess

Neither the broken nose nor the scars on her cheeks diminish her beauty. We do not know who she is, but it is likely that she is a goddess, perhaps a cult statue. She wears a floral crown of painted lotuses; the eyes retain their original color; and there are traces of paint on the lips and hair. She, too, has the appearance of someone emerging from archaic dreams into the world of the living. In a few years the formal curls will give way to heavy hair flowing naturally; the eyebrows will lose their scimitar shapes; and the mouth will grow softer. Then she will be a goddess no longer. For the first time, in Periclean Athens, the gods became human, but this girl is still far from being completely human.

The bronze statuette of a horse, nearly nine inches high, belongs to the same period as the horses on the Vix vase, the general design, even to the little knot on the waistband, being identical. The horses at Vix were arranged in fours, and this very stately horse was originally accompanied by three others and presented as an offering in one of the temples at Olympia. Two of the legs are broken, but the animal is carved on such a monumental scale that we feel no more sense of loss than when we encounter a life-size Apollo without his toes.

The Olympia horse is a masterpiece of sustained energy and self-regarding beauty. There are still elements of the archaic in the body, but the head is alert, eager, wholly self-conscious. There is a rather similar horse with the same stiff upbrushed mane but without the decorative pompon in the Metropolitan Museum in New York.

The griffin head, dating from about 600 B.C., once decorated a bronze tripod. Many of these tripods have been found, including one discovered near Châtillon-sur-Seine in 1846 and then forgotten until the discovery of the Vix vase gave it a new importance. Four griffins with long, serpentine necks rise from the top of the Châtillon tripod, and they are fine and angry beasts, fit guardians of whatever sacred objects they defended. The Olympia griffin is the most perfect specimen which has come to light, far more angry and ferocious than any others. Ferocity here assumes an almost abstract form. The brilliant curves of beak and tongue, the layered ridges above the eyes, the upright ear which seems to be quivering with awareness of imminent danger, the curious fish scales mottling half the head, all these come together to produce an image of uncanny power. This griffin had power to kill.

Bronze statuette of a horse

Griffin head from Olympia

Christ from the Church of the Holy Mother in Prizren

# OHRID AND PRIZREN

In the Middle Ages Ohrid, a small town in southeastern Yugoslavia on the borders of Greece, was a nest of churches, the seat of an important bishopric, and an outpost of Byzantine influence. The most famous of the churches was the Church of the Mother of God, completed in A.D. 1295 with the help of two painters of authentic genius, Eutychius and Michael, whose signatures appear in various parts of the church. To the refinement of Byzantine painting in the thirteenth century they added a human vigor and a human depth of feeling. In painting after painting we see them subtly modifying Byzantine forms to breathe a greater life in them.

Angel fresco from Santa Sophia in Ohrid

When the Turks conquered Macedonia in the fourteenth century, they permitted the Church of the Mother of God to remain open to Christians, the other churches being converted into mosques. These paintings, therefore, were never defaced nor covered with plaster; but since the church was in almost continuous use for more than six centuries, the smoke from candles and holy lamps laid a thick deposit of soot on the walls, and the paintings vanished from sight. The restorers have removed the dirt and the overpainting, and today the frescoes gleam in all their original brightness. In "The Death of the Mother of God" we see Christ attended by a column of weeping angels at His mother's bedside, and we are made sharply aware of the waves of grief beating upwards and around the dark figure of the Virgin on the simple bed.

All over Yugoslavia the ancient churches are being restored and long-lost paintings are being brought to light. Yugoslav experts calculate that about a quarter of the existing churches have been carefully examined, and no one knows how many masterpieces lie under their protective coating of Turkish plaster. Most of these churches are in Serbia, Kosovo-Metohija, and Macedonia, where the Byzantine influence was greatest.

The Church of the Mother of God in Ohrid was built by order of King Milutin, who also built the Church of the Holy Mother in Prizren upon the foundations of an old basilica. The church was completed in A.D. 1307. Under Turkish rule it was converted into a mosque and the frescoes were covered with plaster until the end of World War II, when a vast panorama of bright colors was revealed—altogether five hundred square meters of plaster were removed between 1949 and 1953.

The styles of the Ohrid and Prizren frescoes are profoundly different. The paintings at Ohrid have a robust physical quality, closer to Giotto than to the Byzantine masters. There is an earthiness about them which suggests that the artists employed models for their saints and apostles. It is unlikely that models were used at Prizren, where we are aware of a brutal and monumental power in the designs which seem to have sprung fully formed from the artist's imagination—a vision closer to El Greco than to Giotto. A fierce and unrelenting vigor is the mark of the Prizren Master. The Turks scooped holes in the walls so that the plaster would take hold, but even though these holes sometimes give an effect of whirling snowflakes, we can still appreciate the brilliant and disturbing quality of the painting.

The "Death of the Virgin" from the Church of the Holy Mother in Ohrid

# CONSTANTINOPLE: THE GREAT PALACE

ON the slopes running down from the Hippodrome to the Sea of Marmora lay the Great Palace of the Byzantine Caesars. Every successive Caesar took pride in adding to it. In this city within a city were vast reception halls, churches, libraries, prisons, pavilions, stairways, terraces and towers, all set amid flowering gardens. The great halls were splendid with marble columns, mosaic floors, and statues plundered from all over Greece. Here the Caesars lived in Oriental magnificence until in the twelfth century the Comneni abandoned this palace and built another, equally magnificent, at the other end of the Golden Horn.

Eagle and snake mosaic from the Great Palace of the Byzantine Emperors

Very little is known about the Great Palace, although a large part of it must have survived until the conquest of Constantinople by the Turks in 1453. Recent excavations, conducted on behalf of the Walker Trust of St. Andrews University, have revealed a series of mosaic floors lying over vaults of massive stonework. The stonework belongs to the age of Constantine, but the mosaics would seem to be sixth-century work of the age of Justinian, and therefore contemporary with the building of Hagia Sophia.

Mosaic of a woman carrying a water jar

To the surprise of the archaeologists, all the mosaics proved to be of pagan subjects. Originally they formed a pavement around a colonnaded courtyard a hundred feet square. The scenes depicted in the mosaics were unrelated, and it has been impossible to discover any general theme. The mosaics are all designed against a plain white background; but some of the designs are heraldic, like the great eagle in the coils of a serpent, while others are quietly naturalistic. We see birds flying, peasants milking a goat, and a man leading his two sons on a camel. We see a philosopher sitting on rocks, a woman carrying a heavy wine jar, a boy feeding a donkey. There are hunting scenes, fantastic animals, and circus games. The artist seems to have been permitted to make any design he pleased with no thought of a continuing story, with the result that the mosaic possesses a curiously innocent quality. One suspects that it may have been made for a child.

A boy feeding a donkey from the Great Palace

The artist has been at pains to develop a human quality in his characters. The boy holding the wicker basket to feed the donkey advances gingerly, aware of the sidelong gleam in the donkey's eyes, and not at all certain of his reception; the donkey, however, is completely self-assured. Both donkey and boy seem to be portraits drawn from life.

The mosaic pieces are made of marble chips, colored stones, and brilliant shades of glass in blue, green, and yellow. There are no shadows, no backgrounds, no foregrounds. Everything takes place against a white translucent sky, perhaps to differentiate these curious stories from the New Testament stories which are always told against a golden sky. Probably these mosaics belonged to a wing of the palace where the young princes and princesses grew up, but so far it has been impossible to identify the building.

The mosaic portrait of Theodoros Metochites

# CONSTANTINOPLE: THE CHORA CHURCH

THE Chora Church (Kariye Camii) stands near the Adrianople Gate in the stony back streets of Constantinople, far from the Great Palace of the Emperors. It is not an imposing church, and a visitor might be excused if he passed by without giving it a thought, for the minaret and drab exterior show little promise. From the street there is nothing to suggest that here, during the last years of the Byzantine Empire, an artist painted frescoes and designed mosaics which are among the greatest in the world.

No one knows the name of the artist, but we do know the name of the man who presented the mosaics, and perhaps also the frescoes, to the church. He was Theodoros Metochites, and during the years of his prosperity in the early fourteenth century he was Grand Logothete, or Prime Minister, in the court of Emperor Andronicus II. Poet, astronomer, scientist, commentator on the classics, courtier and ambassador-extraordinary, he was among the most brilliant men of his time. As ambassador, he brought about peace between the Byzantines and the Serbians; as astronomer, he wrote treatises on the Ptolemaic system; and as philosopher, he revived and encouraged the study of Plato and Aristotle. In the end he fell from favor and spent his last days in the church as a simple monk.

We see him dressed in his official robes, a patterned gown of blue silk with flowers and leaves embroidered in gold, wearing a soaring cap of office, as he kneels at the feet of Christ and presents the blue-domed Church of the Chora to Him. The background is a blaze of gold. The inscription, recording the name and high position of the donor, is written

Fresco of the Resurrection of the Dead from the Chora Church

XC

in the space behind him. With his dark beard, long nose, and untroubled gaze, he has the look of a man accustomed to power and influence, with very little humility in him. He is very proud of his church.

He had reason to be proud, for the church which he restored and decorated between A.D. 1303 and 1320 has a new lightness, a new grace and delicacy. The brooding heaviness of so many Byzantine mosaics is absent. It is as though spring had come again to reinvigorate the ancient forms of saints and worshipers. With the discovery of these mosaics we see the art of Byzantium putting forth new shoots and adapting itself to changing circumstances. The Chora Church is almost exactly contemporary with Giotto's great Arena Chapel at Padua, but there is a heaviness and sturdiness in Giotto's figures which we rarely find in the work of the Chora Master.

Look, for example, at the Resurrection of the Dead painted in the apse, which is recognizably by the artist who designed the mosaics. Christ has harrowed Hell, broken the locks, smashed down the gates, and thrown a chain round the neck of Satan. He strides triumphant over Hell, and by His power brings Adam and Eve to life again. If Adam looks uncommonly like Michelangelo's God in the Sistine Chapel, this is no fault of the painter, who died a hundred and fifty years before Michelangelo was born. Adam does not so much rise out of the tomb as hurl himself toward Christ. The Baptist points the way, while David and Solomon look on, their golden crowns merging imperceptibly with their golden halos. Abel, with his shepherd's crook, watches impassively the resurrection of his father Adam, while the blessed dead cluster behind him. But it is the figure of Christ in diaphanous white vestments, set daringly against a white and blue mandorla, which commands our attention, for the swift beauty of His movement and the majestic power radiating from Him. The mandorla takes the form of a star-studded eggshell, and as He stands there, emerging out of creation, impatient to lift the weight of death from the earth, He is both sail and anchor, soaring and yet rooted to the earth. Below Him lie the *disjecta membra* of Hell, a great jumble of bars, bolts, hinges, nails, keys, locks, and doorposts flickering with blue fire. The setting is traditional. These twisted rocks form the conventional background of innumerable Byzantine paintings and mosaics. What is not traditional is the astonishing vividness and immediacy of the composition. This is one of the greatest of all Christian paintings.

Until recently, the Resurrection of the Dead was hidden beneath the coat of plaster which covered it ever since the Turks transformed the church into a mosque. In places the plaster was wearing thin, and here and there one could make out a few ghostly shapes, like pale faces peering through snow and ice. The work of restoration was undertaken by Dr. Paul Underwood of the Byzantine Institute. Gently, inch by inch, first washing the plaster away with water, then chipping at the last vestiges of plaster with orange sticks and dental instruments, he was able to restore the painting to a state of almost original freshness. Small fragments from the left side of the face of Christ have been lost, but only a trained observer would notice it.

The same elaborate and careful methods were used with the mosaics, with only water or very light solutions of acid being applied to the plaster. The work was not ended when the plaster was removed and the mosaics were cleaned, for some of the *tesserae* were loose and had to be firmly embedded. This painstaking labor, which went on at a snail's pace, had its own rewards, for the restorers, seeing the work of great artists coming to life in their hands, were able to share something of the excitement of creation.

At one time the entire narthex and exonarthex and large areas of the interior of the church were covered with mosaics. Some of these mosaics have been lost, with the result that there are gaps in the continuing story. There is no Last Supper, no Betrayal, no Crucifixion: presumably these were destroyed at the time of the Turkish conquest. The Nativity of Christ is represented, and the Journey to Bethlehem, but immediately afterwards we are transported to the Feeding of the Five Thousand and the Miracle at Cana. The life of the Virgin, as related in the Protoevangelion of St. James, is told in considerable detail. Joachim prays in the desert, and there is the familiar scene of Joachim and Anne embracing at the gate of Jerusalem. The lunette showing the birth of the Virgin is followed by one depicting the first nine steps of the Virgin. A female servant wearing a blue gown, her face framed in a rose-red scarf billowing in the mysterious wind of God, helps the Virgin on her way. The servant almost dominates the picture. She wears a coronet like the new moon in her hair, and there is a curious suggestion of classical influence in the billowing scarf—a similar scarf is worn by sea nymphs and by Venus in classical paintings. The Virgin has the face of a demure ten-year-old, wiser than her years. Her hands are spread apart, and she totters a little as she makes her first tentative steps. In this way, very tenderly, she enters into holiness.

So it is with all the remaining mosaics. There is a freshness, a lightness, a kind of laughing gaiety in all of them. The traditional scenes are observed with eyes unencumbered by tradition. Whoever he was—and there is no vestige of a signature in any of the mosaics, nor is he mentioned in any surviving documents—the master of the Chora Church must be ranked among the great masters of the world.

Detail of the mosaic of the first steps of the Virgin

# CONSTANTINOPLE: HAGIA SOPHIA

WHEN the Emperor Justinian in the incredible space of six years built the cathedral of Hagia Sophia on the ruins of a cathedral which had been burned to the ground by rioting fanatics, he could not prevent himself from crying out: "Glory be to God who hath counted me to perform so great a work. Solomon, I have surpassed thee!"

He had surpassed his utmost hopes, and he had surpassed Solomon. His architect, Anthemius, had succeeded in supporting a vast dome on two semidomes, and these in turn were supported on three semidomes, giving an effect of spaciousness hitherto undreamed of. The decoration was as magnificent as the architecture. The dome was painted blue and studded with stars. Marble and porphyry columns were plundered from the temples of Diana of the Ephesians and of Zeus at Olympia, and even the Parthenon at Athens was not spared. Columns of Syene granite which had long ago been floated down the Nile and set up at Baalbek were hauled down to make a second journey to Constantinople. Every art and artifice known to the Byzantines was placed at the service of the new cathedral. Justinian commanded that the walls should represent the fields of paradise and the dome should suggest the infinite spaces of heaven, and he accomplished exactly what he set out to do. He had built the greatest church in Christendom.

Hagia Sophia, completed in A.D. 537, still stands, but nearly all the jewels and precious stones and mosaics which decorated it in the time of Justinian have vanished. Successive Emperors have made offerings of gold plate and then melted them down, put up memorials to themselves and then destroyed them. The modern visitor is aware of an immense calm spaciousness and a kind of bleakness, and this bleakness is increased rather than diminished by the presence of the great marble and porphyry columns and the huge balloons inscribed with Arabic prayers which now hang from the ceiling to prove that the Moslems are in full possession of Hagia Sophia.

The years of barrenness are coming to an end. Patient explorers have been chipping away at the plaster with which the Turks covered the domes and walls when the cathedral was converted into a mosque, and one after another brilliant mosaics are coming to light. The visitor wanders through the empty cavernous cathedral, and suddenly, high up on one of the semidomes, he sees the Virgin in a golden glory, trembling in the sunlight filtering through high windows, silent and motionless, but continually in movement, so remote that she seems to be lost in the unreachable heavens, and so close that she seems to be coming across the room.

We owe the salvaging and cleaning of these mosaics very largely to the late Dr. Thomas Whittemore, the Boston archaeologist who founded the Byzantine Institute in 1934. With extraordinary single-mindedness and enthusiasm he dedicated himself to Hagia Sophia, spending endless hours on the high scaffolding examining each minute stone or fragment of glass as it appeared. He was a forceful man, with his own theories about the development of mosaic art, and not all scholars were in agreement with him; but his work on the mosaics of Hagia Sophia was in its own way as important as Schliemann's work at Troy and Mycenae.

The mosaics he uncovered range over four hundred years of Byzantine history. The panel showing Christ flanked by an Emperor and Empress, on the east wall of the south gallery, dates from about A.D. 1030 and provides a wonderful illustration of imperial faking. The Empress Zoe is depicted on the right, the Emperor Constantine IX Monomachus on the left, and their names and titles are inscribed above their halos. Dr. Whittemore observed, however, that the inscription above the Emperor's head had been tampered with, and a careful examination of the Emperor's features showed that a new head had been substituted for an older one not long after the mosaic was made.

Now the Empress Zoe, the last Empress of the Macedonian dynasty, came to the throne when she was over fifty. She was a small, strange, timid woman, who had lived all her life in the shadow of her father, the hearty and half-savage Constantine VIII, who had forced her on his deathbed

Christ flanked by donor portraits of Constantine Monomachos and Zoe

to marry the sixty-year-old Romanus Argyrus, the highest civil dignitary in the government of Constantinople. Romanus objected. He was already married. Told that he would be blinded if he refused the Emperor's command, he divorced his wife, married Zoe, and was elevated to the purple under the title of Romanus III Argyrus. Zoe soon wearied of him and took as her lover a handsome youth called Michael, the brother of one of the palace eunuchs. After a reign of six years Romanus III Argyrus died not very mysteriously in his bath, and Michael became Emperor. He was in his twenties, and the Empress was thirty years older, but the marriage might have endured if Michael had not been an epileptic subject to sporadic attacks of religious mania and remorse for having murdered his predecessor. He built the handsome Church of St. Cosmas and St. Damian, venerated the relics of saints, kissed the ulcers of the sick, educated prostitutes to a life of virtue, and founded almshouses. He was a just and kindly ruler, but his attacks of religious mania grew ever more violent, and in A.D. 1041, after a reign of seven years, he abruptly left the court and retired to a monastery, dying a few days later, probably of poison. The Empress Zoe took as her third husband Constantine Monomachus, a high official in the civil government. She had a deep affection for him, for she allowed him to bring his mistress to court and permitted her to receive the honors due to an Empress. Constantine was a dull-witted spendthrift with a talent for survival, dying of old age after a reign of fourteen years.

Though Constantine is represented in the mosaic, Dr. Whittemore came to the conclusion that it was originally made when Romanus III Argyrus was on the throne. The tampering with the letters of the inscription is quite obvious, and of the two former Emperors only Romanus exactly fills the available space. We see Christ in a rich blue gown against a gold background. Constantine offers a moneybag, representing his worldly treasure; Zoe offers a scroll. Constantine glowers, and Zoe smiles mysteriously, gazing not at Christ but at the jeweled Bible on His knees.

About a hundred years later, in the same gallery, a rather similar mosaic was made to celebrate the Emperor John II Comnenus and the Empress Irene, daughter of King Ladislas of Hungary. The Virgin stands in the center with the Child on her knees. Once more the Emperor offers his moneybag and the Empress presents a scroll. John was a brilliant and versatile ruler, Irene a gentle and persuasive Empress, who built almshouses and hospitals. It is related of her that she fell at the feet of her

Mosaic portrait of the Empress Irene

husband in tears when she found she was unable to complete her charitable work. The portrait of her, inscribed *Eirene Augusta,* is simpler, stronger, and altogether more lifelike than the portrait of Zoe. With her red hair and pink cheeks, she gives the impression of a woman perfectly in command of herself. Her vestments are a blaze of gold and scarlet, studded with jewels. The sharp linear manner is typical of the early years of the Comnene period.

Among the very greatest of Dr. Whittemore's discoveries was the mosaic known as the "Deesis Panel," which came to light in 1933. This enormous panel—originally it was eighteen feet high, but the greater part of the lower portion has perished—represents the Virgin and St. John interceding with Christ for the sins of the world. Only the head and shoulders of the Virgin remain, and the heads and busts of Christ and the Baptist. Christ is serene majesty, but there is a humanity and gentleness in His expression rare in Byzantine art, and the yearning gaze of the Baptist is expressed with a delicacy and controlled violence which are even rarer. The bronze-colored hair sweeps backward in waves of power; the darker beard is tangled with despair. It is a portrait overflowing with human feeling, far removed from the stiff, hieratic portraits which appear only too frequently in Byzantine art.

The "Deesis Panel" is one of the supreme achievements of the Byzantine artists, to be compared with the great figure of God in Majesty at Daphni. The name of the artist is unknown, and there is considerable speculation about the date of its composition. Dr. Whittemore suggested A.D. 1100. At various times Dr. David Talbot Rice has suggested A.D. 1150, 1190, and even 1270. Such differences are a tribute to the genius of the mosaicist, defying tradition and inventing new methods in order to convey his vision of the world.

John the Baptist from the "Deesis Panel"

Artemis of the Ephesians

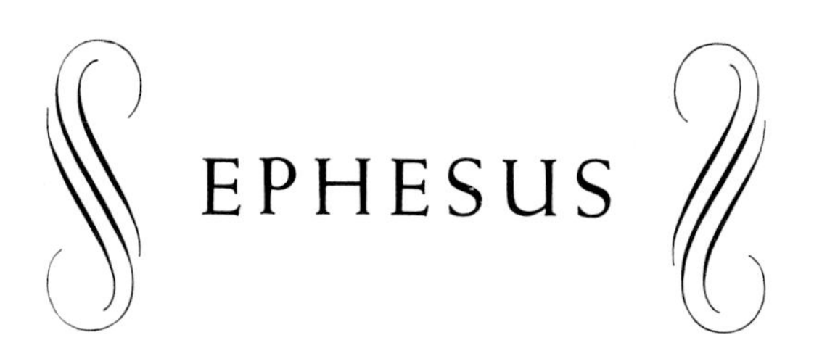

# EPHESUS

IN its long heyday Ephesus was one of the wonders of the world. It was the leading seaport of Asia Minor, ranking as the chief of the twelve Ionian cities along the coast, famous for its poets, its philosophers, and the luxurious dresses of its women. The temple of Artemis was 425 feet long, with 127 columns 60 feet high—in its time the largest temple in the world. According to Greek tradition, Ephesus was founded in the eleventh century B.C. It survived until the fourteenth century A.D., and therefore had a life of twenty-five centuries. Now of that vast city there are only tumbled ruins on the foothills.

Archaeologists seem to choose instinctively the sites which suggest their own national characteristics. So the French have explored Delos, the island of light, while the Americans and the British find themselves more at home in ancient Athens; the Germans are happiest among the gaunt ruins of Olympia, and the Italians among the splendors of Cyrene and Phaistos. For nearly seventy years the Austrians have been excavating at Ephesus, where Heraclitus walked and luxury was celebrated. Ephesus was another Vienna—rich, elegant, and profoundly contemplative.

Recent excavations under the direction of Dr. Franz Miltner of the Austrian Archaeological Institute have led to important discoveries, especially in the center of the ancient city, where they have succeeded in unearthing Hellenistic, Roman, and Byzantine remains. An elegant bathhouse with well-appointed brothels, begun during the reign of Domitian and restored three centuries later during the reign of Theodosius, testifies to the tenacity of Ephesian institutions. Behind this bathhouse the Austrians discovered the highway leading to the city hall. This highway, flanked with colonnades, shops, and marble statues, and decorated with mosaic pavements, suggested a standard of luxury which was equaled in antiquity perhaps only by the main highway of Antioch. Beside the city hall was found the sanctuary of Hestia Boulaia, the goddess who presided over the counsels of the city fathers. Here they found two statues of Artemis Ephesia, "Diana of the Ephesians," one twice life-size, the other life-size. Both are astonishing works of art.

According to Greek mythology, Artemis was the virgin sister of Apollo, armed with a silver bow, and like Apollo she possessed the power to kill at random and to bring light and order into a chaotic world. But the Artemis beloved by the Ephesians was essentially a fertility goddess always represented as many-breasted; her emblems were lions, griffins, and stags, and she was attended by eunuch priests. We have only to compare her with Brauronian Artemis to see that she had almost nothing in common with the goddess worshiped in Attica and Sparta. She was, in fact, an ancient Asiatic divinity who was already being worshiped in Ionia when the Greeks settled there.

This Asiatic goddess is represented with great strength and beauty, especially in the smaller of the two statues found by the Austrian expedition. The face has a commanding aspect; she is naked to the waist except for her serpent collar and the signs of the zodiac on her chest, signifying that she is also a goddess of the seasons and of time; and there is nothing in the least disturbing about her multitudinous breasts, which resemble a cluster of heavy grapes or sumptuous fruit hanging from a tree. She wears a close-fitting skirt, patterned with lions, griffins, and stags. This skirt ends in a frill like a fish's tail, and she is clearly related to the ancient fish-goddesses, who were also purveyors of fertility. Yet what is most remarkable about the statue is the imperial grandeur of the goddess, who wears the tiara of the emperors, and who never for a moment forgets that she rules over a teeming city. This fish-goddess with the many breasts should be barbaric and unpleasing. In fact, the artist has succeeded in rendering a portrait of a divinity which is curiously convincing.

# HALICARNASSUS

IN August 1953 some sponge fishermen diving off the small town of Bodrum, the ancient Halicarnassus, found the upper part of a bronze statue of a woman of extraordinary grace and beauty, and with great difficulty they succeeded in bringing it to shore. Except for a large wound on the top of the head, the statue was undamaged, though thickly encrusted with a grayish coating of fossilized sea creatures and there was something which looked uncommonly like a small gray sea serpent coiling round her neck. The face of the statue was miraculously preserved. The Turkish fishermen were not quite sure who she was, and they very sensibly colored her cheeks and lips with red paint to bring her back to life. In this painted state she was seen by an English archaeologist, Professor George Bean of Istanbul University, who was traveling in Asia Minor with his sister. When the professor pointed out that they had discovered a statue of the goddess Demeter, of surpassing beauty, from the finest workshops of Athens, the Turkish fishermen rather shamefacedly washed off the paint.

The Demeter of Bodrum belongs to the great series of recent finds which includes the Zeus of Artemision. No comparable statue of Demeter is known. The goddess mother of the cornfields is shown mourning for her lost daughter Persephone, who was snatched away every year by Hades, god of the underworld, to spend the winter months in the nether world. According to Greek mythology, Demeter abandoned her home in Olympus and spent these months wandering the earth searching for her lost daughter, and her shrine at Eleusis, near Athens, was among the most sumptuous of all the shrines in Greece.

The Demeter of Bodrum is larger than life, quivering with the intensity of her grief, overwhelmed with the agony of her sorrow as she gazes sightlessly at a world which remains incomprehensible so long as her daughter is removed from her. She is the sorrowing mother of all time, and very close in feeling to the Virgin at the foot of the Cross.

No one knows how she came to be in the sea. She must have been made towards the end of the fifth century or in the early fourth century B.C., and then shipped from Athens to some town on the coast of Asia Minor where a temple had been especially erected for her. The most famous Greek statues were usually copied, but no copy of this statue is known to exist. Professor Bean has suggested that no copies were made because it was lost in the shipwreck shortly after being made. He has also suggested that it may have been intended for the temple at Cnidus, and that the well-known Demeter of Cnidus, now in the British Museum, may have been a replacement for the statue lost at sea.

Soon after its discovery the statue was taken to Istanbul University, where it was carefully cleaned. Today it is quite easily the most beautiful object in the museum at Smyrna.

The Demeter of Bodrum

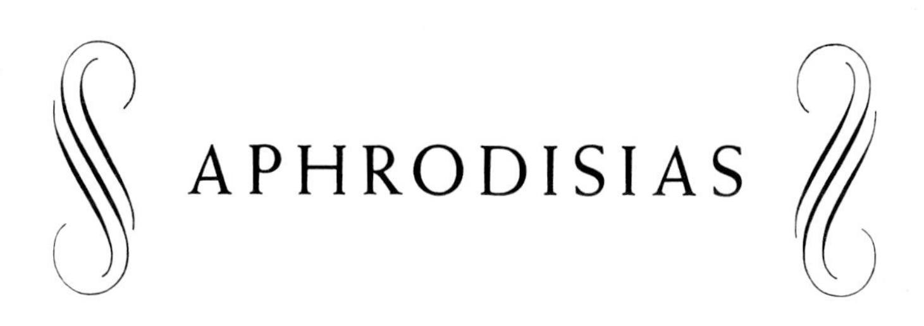

# APHRODISIAS

IN a wide and beautiful valley in southwestern Turkey, a hundred miles from the Aegean Sea, there is a small village called Geyre, famous for its almonds. The villagers are quietly prosperous, for the valley is well-watered, rich in springs, with good farmlands and orchards. In all of Turkey there is hardly another valley as lush as this.

For centuries the villagers of Geyre have been accustomed to living among ruins. Everywhere they looked they saw fallen columns, broken parapets, and other vestiges of ancient temples. Outside the village, across the open fields, there stands a marble stadium nearly 900 feet long, capable of seating perhaps 30,000 spectators. If all the villagers were gathered together in it, they would form no more than a small brown spot in its white immensity.

Once, where Geyre now stands, there was a great and gleaming city called Aphrodisias. The city was sacred to "immortal Aphrodite, the rainbow-throned daughter of Zeus." No one knows why Aphrodite, who arose from the sea, should have been celebrated so far inland, and very little is known of the city's history, which is rarely mentioned until Hellenistic times, and then only briefly. Far from the coast, and at some distance from the great military roads, Aphrodisias seems to have lived quietly and peacefully, almost outside of history.

Little is known of Aphrodisias except that it produced a famous school of sculpture, and pieces signed by Aphrodisian artists have been found in Greece and Italy. There were marble quarries nearby: the marble has a rich milky clarity. The city seems to have come into existence in the third

Ruins of the Basilica at Aphrodisias

century B.C., when Asia Minor was being ruled by the successors of Alexander the Great, and probably reached its greatest extent under the rule of the Romans in the first and second centuries A.D. Living on the export of marble and finished sculptures, it seems to have retained a characteristically Greek character to the end.

The jewel of the city was the temple of Aphrodite, which lies some seven hundred feet north of the Acropolis. Most of the fallen columns have been replaced during the recent excavations, giving an idea of the quite extraordinary beauty of the original. In the fifth century A.D. this temple was converted into a Byzantine basilica by the simple process of dismantling the inner walls comprising the *cella* of the pagan temple and using the bricks for building the outer walls of the basilica, only a few columns being displaced. In time, the city of Aphrodite became Stauropolis, the city of the Holy Cross, the center of an important bishopric. With the conquest of Asia Minor by the Turks it fell gradually into decay.

Aphrodisias was not forgotten. The memory of a gleaming marble city lost somewhere in southwestern Turkey haunted Renaissance Europe, and it is possible that Aphrodisias is the mysterious Calindra mentioned by Leonardo da Vinci in his imaginary account of a voyage among the

Relief fragment of Zoilos crowned by Honor

Taurus Mountains. Elizabethan seamen, collecting statues among the islands of the eastern Mediterranean and off the coast of Turkey, seem to have visited the site; but the first comprehensive description of Aphrodisias in modern times was made in 1740 by Richard Pococke, the English traveler who was also the first to give a comprehensive account of the Valley of the Kings in Egypt. Later the Society of Dilettanti, founded in 1734 by a small group of English gentlemen of taste and devoted antiquaries, published a volume of architectural drawings with an account of the antiquities of Aphrodisias. Then for a hundred years the city was forgotten. There were brief French expeditions in 1904 and 1905, and an even briefer Italian one in 1937. In 1961 the Department of Classics of New York University financed an expedition under the direction of Professor Jotham Johnson with Professor Kenan Erim serving as field director, and for the first time a full-scale archaeological excavation was started.

The first year of the excavations was largely devoted to clearing the site of the temple of Aphrodite and re-erecting the fallen columns. The most important discoveries were made on the northeast wall of the Byzantine fortifications on the Acropolis, where large slabs of a monumental relief had been accidentally discovered in 1956. More slabs came to light, enabling the archaeologists to give meaning to the entire relief. One of the slabs found in 1956 depicted a headless Aphrodite; during the course of the 1961 excavations the missing head was recovered.

Relief fragment of Eternity represented as an old man

Relief with a headless Aphrodite found in 1956

The monumental relief was dedicated to a certain Zoilos, most probably one of the Roman-appointed governors of the city. On two panels he now appears headless, but it is possible that the heads will yet come to light. It is also possible that two more panels will be found with the figure of Zoilos, for the monument was probably in the form of a square with Zoilos being crowned by different allegorical figures on each of the four sides. Zoilos and the allegorical figures are identified by inscriptions in a beautiful Greek script. We see him being offered crowns by Aphrodite, by Demos (the People), by Timé (Honor), and by Aion (Eternity), who is represented as an old man sitting on a lion-legged chair. The features of Aion are purely Hellenistic, though he must have been carved in the first or second century A.D.

The head of Aphrodite found in 1961

The Aphrodite is the finest piece so far discovered at Aphrodisias. Like the Victory of Samothrace, she is shown alighting on the earth, her draperies still swirling round her, still filled with air; and there is a whirling scarf round her head forming an immense halo. What is chiefly remarkable about the relief, even in its mutilated state, is the freshness of the modeling of the bare shoulders and breasts, and the rich folds of her gown. Her legs have been blackened by the soil, and the head has not yet been attached to the neck, but how vivid she is! with what grace she alights on the earth! and what a tangle of rich draperies float round her! She is breathtakingly alive. She seems to have leapt down from the heavens singing.

The head of Aphrodite, found in 1961, wears the civic crown to emphasize her role as guardian of the city. No existing photographs do her justice, for the head has a sweetness and serenity in keeping with the gentle gaiety of the body.

Excavations at Aphrodisias are continuing. There are few places where so much treasure is likely to be found.

Painted terra-cotta duck from Gordion

# GORDION

UNTIL recently the Phrygians were among the more mysterious nations which inhabited Asia Minor. Homer refers to them as allies of the Trojans, and Priam's queen, Hecuba, was a Phrygian princess. It was known that kings of the dynasty of Midas ruled from the capital city of Gordion on the Sangarius River, and many legends were told of these wealthy and powerful kings who assumed control over large areas of the Hittite Empire. The Greeks told the story of how Midas received from Silenus the gift of turning everything he touched into gold. Even his food turned to gold, and he was in danger of dying when Dionysus ordered him to bathe in the river Pactolus. Then the curse was lifted, and ever since that day the river has had an abundance of gold in its sands.

This pleasant story testifies to the wealth pouring into the treasuries of the ruling dynasty of Gordion. From the twelfth to the seventh century B.C., Phrygia remained the dominant power in Asia Minor, growing in wealth and influence, until the kingdom was destroyed by Cimmerian nomads advancing from the region of the Sea of Azov. They vanished after looting and setting fire to the capital city, and the vacuum was filled by the Persians who extended their rule until it embraced the whole of Asia Minor. By classical times, Gordion and the dynasty of Midas were little more than dim memories.

Today only a few Phrygian monuments remain above ground, the most impressive being the "Midas Monument" at Yazilikaya, where, carved in the living rock, is the representation of a gable end façade of a Phrygian palace ornamented with intricate patterns in relief. These patterns, which are continually repeated, would be more suitable to wood or glazed tiles or carpets, and it seems reasonably clear that the designer of the monument was imitating one of these materials on the rock surface. We shall see later that the pattern must have had a peculiar significance for the Phrygian kings.

Archaeologists, remembering the legends of King Midas, have for a long time been drawn to the burial mounds in Phrygian territory. There are some hundreds of these mounds scattered from Cappadocia to the Black Sea and the Aegean. The most tempting were the mounds at Gordion, the capital, and therefore the place where valuable objects were most likely to be found. One mound, 165 feet high, was especially attractive, for it evidently contained the burial chamber of one of the Phrygian Kings or an important member of his family. But how does one find a small chamber buried within a mountain?

The problem was finally solved during an expedition led by Dr. Rodney Young under the auspices of the University of Pennsylvania. A series of excavations in Gordion begun in 1950 permitted the archaeologists to study the great mound from all directions. For five years they worked on the smaller mounds. Fourteen of these were excavated between 1950 and 1951, often with discouraging results. The first major break-through came

Gold bracelet from a tomb at Gordion

with the discovery of some gold and electrum jewelry in some mid-sixth-century tumuli where the bodies had been cremated, the jewelry being found among the ashes. The gold bracelet with the lion heads is almost certainly of Persian origin. It would seem that the survivors of the Cimmerian massacres had continued to live in Gordion, coming more and more under Persian influence. This bracelet is one of the few gold objects found in a region reputed to be rich in gold.

The archaeologists were still plagued with the difficulty of finding the small tomb chamber, which was rarely if ever placed directly beneath the dome of the mound. Such tombs were usually wooden chambers surrounded by a great thickness of stone rubble enclosed within a containing wall. If a robber succeeded in locating the chamber and broke through the containing wall, he would as likely as not be smothered to death by the fall of stone. So there were two problems facing the archaeologists: how to find the chamber, and how to break into it?

A particularly ingenious solution to the first problem was designed by Dr. Young. A light, portable oil-drilling rig was procured, and soundings were made in order to map out the stone-capped roof of the burial chamber. Soundings of the great mound were taken during the fall of 1955 and the summer of 1956. The chamber was found to be a hundred feet in diameter and located to the southwest of the center of the mound.

Meanwhile, in the spring of 1956, a practice drill resulted in the discovery of a child's tomb in a tumulus about forty feet high. Of the body nothing remained except a few teeth, but these were sufficient to tell the age of the child—about four to five years old—and the furnishings, though heavily damaged by the fall of rubble from the capped roof, showed that the child must have been a princely member of the royal dynasty. The body had been lying on a wooden bed; and the same curious designs which appear on the Midas Monument at Yazilikaya were found with variations in the wood inlays forming the bed. Some purple-red fibers hinted at a purple cushion, and there were signs that draperies had once hung round the tomb chamber. The most imposing object was a heavy bronze caldron. It was neither as large nor as finely modeled as the enormous Greek vase found in the tomb chamber at Vix, but it served the same emblematic and ritual purpose; and the tomb chamber at Vix, near Paris, was constructed in very much the same way as this tomb in the heart of Anatolia.

The child was evidently a prince rather than a princess, for his toys included wooden lions and horses. Perhaps the most surprising discovery was a shallow bowl of clear molded glass shaped like a modern fruit dish: It is the earliest known vessel of molded glass. But the design of the Phrygian fruit dish is scarcely more interesting than the design of a modern fruit dish. What really excited the archaeologists were the painted earthenware jars, especially a pair of jars shaped like plump ducks. They are a brilliant yellow and covered with geometrical designs imitating feathers in soft black. The necks and beaks serve as spouts, and the tail feathers form the handles. These ducks would make admirable teapots! But what is still more striking about them is their wonderfully friendly, well-bred air. They have a ripeness which suggests that they were made during a time of prosperity by artists who thoroughly enjoyed life and the making of pottery.

The excavation of the young prince's tomb was only a trial run for the larger undertaking. By this time the great mound had been thoroughly explored by oil-drills, and the archaeologists knew exactly where the burial chamber was to be found. They had two alternatives: either to sink a vertical shaft from the top of the mound, or to drive a tunnel into the mound from one side. For various reasons they chose the second alternative, and miners were imported to do the work. In twenty-five days, working around the clock, they carried the tunnel right up to a stone wall which comprised the outer defenses of the tomb. The wall was breached, and immediately a mass of small stones poured into the tunnel; but this was exactly what they had expected, for they knew from previous excavations that the burial chamber would be protected by thick layers of rubble. What they had not expected was the continual rain of rubble, which lasted for a whole week. At the end of this time, when the rubble was carted away, they could see the outer wooden wall of the tomb chamber, made up of horizontal balks of juniper two feet thick. It remained only to break through this wall, and then to enter the burial chamber.

It did not happen quite like this, however, for when they bored through the wooden wall with an auger, they discovered more stones on the other side. Stone wall, rubble; wood wall, rubble. No one knew how many sandwiches of wall and rubble they would find. Dr. Rodney Young describes the next step of the assault on the tomb chamber:

> There was nothing to do but cut a window through the wall big enough to show what lay within. As the auger had predicted,

> the window showed only more stone rubble. This time, however, we were not held long in suspense; after only about an hour enough rubble had been taken out to reveal the face of a second wooden wall, here made of nicely squared and fitted timbers rather than rough logs. The auger was at hand and bored through the wood without encountering stone at the other side; it was now certain that the tomb was intact and the roof unbroken! A small window was cut through the inner wall, big enough to insert only the head and one arm, with a flashlight. The staff took turns at looking in; the tomb was large, the atmosphere dense, the flashlight weak. Among the wonders thus seen were a chariot, and a stuffed alligator! *

Later, when flood lamps were brought up and the interior of the tomb was illuminated, nearly the whole floor seemed to be gleaming with brilliant peacock-blue objects. These were ancient bronze vessels which had acquired a rich patina over the ages. The tomb had not been robbed. The King still lay on a great four-poster bed with his head toward the east. He wore a skirt of leather ornamented with bronze studs and a sleeved upper-garment fastened with bronze safety pins. Most of the leather skirt had perished, as had most of the upper garment of cloth, while the coverlet of wool and linen of twenty thicknesses which lay over him was reduced to threads. He was a small man, about five feet two inches tall, and about sixty years of age. From radio-carbon tests on wood from the burial chamber it was possible to suggest a date for the burial. The unknown King was placed in his tomb about 743 B.C.

* Rodney S. Young, "The Gordion Tomb," *The Bulletin of the University Museum of the University of Pennsylvania,* Fall, 1958, pp. 6–7.

bearded angel from the bronze caldron

The furniture consisted of nine three-legged boxwood tables, three gigantic copper caldrons on iron tripods, some 167 bronze bowls of various kinds, and two inlaid wooden screens which may have once served as backdrops for the King's thrones. Originally the bowls, which now littered the floor, had rested on the tables, which had collapsed. The caldrons were especially impressive. They were ornamented with angels, winged figures bearing the heads of bearded men or young women. Their faces are studies in angelic calm. The hair ripples like basketwork, and the full beards of the men are engraved with curls. Their eyes are closed, and perhaps they are dead, but they smile mysteriously.

The inlaid wooden screens were in an almost perfect state of preservation. They were made of dark yew with light inlays of boxwood, ingeniously tongued and grooved together, with patterns reminiscent of the Midas Monument at Yazilakaya. Herodotus mentions that King Midas offered an elaborate wooden throne to the temple of Apollo in Delphi, and commentators have long wondered why he would offer anything so simple as a wooden throne, when other kings offered objects in pure gold. The explanation lay in the tomb at Gordion. Just such a throne as this must have been offered to the god.

Bronze buckets ornamented with ram's and lion's heads were found, but these were of Assyrian workmanship, as we know from similar vessels found in the Khorsabad of Sargon II. Beside the King's bed there was found a linen bag containing a collection of 145 bronze brooches and safety pins, and all of these were in the characteristic Phrygian style. Within the tomb, works from Assyria and Phrygia lay side by side, testifying to a close connection between the two nations.

With the discovery of the Gordion tomb, Phrygia emerges into history. For the first time it is beginning to be possible to assess the character and the skills of an almost forgotten people, now shown to have possessed a high standard of culture and to have been among the leaders of civilization in their time. Soon more excavations will reveal the extent of their culture. Meanwhile, archaeologists are faced with a puzzle: Why did the King of a country famous for its gold have not one gold vessel in his tomb?

Arriving in Gordion, Alexander the Great was told of an intricate knot which could only be unraveled by the man destined to conquer the world. Alexander unraveled it by simply cutting it through with his sword. In much the same way, by slicing into the grave mounds at Gordion, modern archaeologists are going about the business of conquering an ancient and little-known world.

Bronze caldron from the Great Tumulus at Gordion

An inlaid wooden throne screen

Colossal head of Antiochus I from Nemrud Dagh

# NEMRUD DAGH

SOME seven thousand feet above sea level in the Anti-Taurus mountains of Turkey there is a conical hill guarding the tomb of Antiochus I of Commagene. He was a brilliant monarch, who owed the survival of his kingdom to the need for a buffer state between Parthia and the Roman vassal-states in Asia Minor. The geographer Strabo says he ruled over "a small, but fertile kingdom." It was, in fact, one of the smallest states which ever occupied an important place in history, deriving its power from its strategic position astride the ancient trade routes between the Orient and the West. The King claimed descent from the Achaemenid Emperors of Persia and from Alexander the Great. His father was King Mithradates Kallinikos, and his mother was Loadicea Thea Philadelphia, a Seleucid Princess.

Long before he died, Antiochus I prepared a funeral monument for himself of unexampled splendor. The monument took the form of a great artificial cone on the summit of a mountain, with courtyards and terraces on the east and west dominated by the figures of the protecting gods, among whom he included himself. Processional ways led to the tomb, and along these were inscriptions carved on steles proclaiming the terrible fate reserved for desecrators. Other inscriptions proclaim that the tomb or *hierothesion* stood "at the topmost ridge of his kingdom in closest proximity to the heavenly throne of Zeus." His mortal remains were to be enclosed in the tomb, but his soul "would ascend into the heavenly spheres of Zeus there to live for unending eternity." And if these statements were not sufficiently ambitious, he hinted that his tomb would become the meeting place of the gods: "I have undertaken to make this holy place a common throneroom for all the gods."

So this great royal tomb came into being among the remote mountains of southeastern Turkey, and Antiochus clearly intended that continual worship should be paid there. He endowed the sanctuary with royal estates, staffed it with priests and musicians, and decreed that twice a month "for everlasting" special prayers should be sung in his honor. The two days corresponded to his birthday and the day he ascended to the throne. Though we know the exact days on which these events took place —he was born on January 16 and ascended to the throne on July 10—we do not know the years. He seems to have died about 34 B.C. and to have planned his tomb some thirty years earlier, for a remarkable lion relief found in the debris of the western courtyard is decorated with astral symbols which have been interpreted by Dr. Otto Neugebauer of Brown University as indicating the 7th day of July, 61 or 62 B.C. In 62 B.C. he was confirmed in his kingdom by Pompey, and the Lion Horoscope may very well be the commemorative stele for the foundation of the tomb sanctuary.

The modern visitor, making the difficult journey to the heights of Nemrud Dagh, finds himself at last in a wild exhilarating landscape. Seen from a distance the tomb gleams like a shimmering snowcap. As the traveler approaches the whiteness vanishes, and the snowcap becomes an immense conical rubble of brown stones. All except one of the great guardian gods have lost their heads in the earthquakes which have periodically convulsed the mountain, but the sense of splendor and exaltation remains.

The east terrace at Nemrud Dagh

What is especially remarkable is the relationship between the seated figures of the gods and the high mound behind them. The setting, the way the gods are shown sitting on their thrones close to the skyline, and their dimensions which seem to have been worked out mathematically to give the maximum impression of power and domination—all these things have breath-taking rightness. Even now, though the heads are mostly tumbled in the debris, these statues give an impression of quivering life.

The statues, which were twenty-five to thirty feet high, reflect a curious mingling of the cultures of Greece and Persia, with overtones of ancient Hittite influence. On the left, as one faces them, is Apollo-Mithras-Helios-Mercury, representing the power of the sun. Then comes Fortuna-Tyche, tutelary goddess of Commagene, wearing a crown of fruit on her head, the symbol of fertility. Then come Zeus-Ahuramazda, the largest of all, with Antiochus I beside him, and Hercules-Artagnes-Ares on the extreme right. On the terrace immediately below Zeus-Ahuramazda there are the remains of a Greek sacrificial altar and a Persian fire altar. Great eagles and lions flank the row of colossi, and gaze out towards the fire altar.

Colossal head of Hercules from the west terrace

Claiming descent from the Persians through his father and from the Greeks through his mother, Antiochus was determined that the statues of the gods should represent the two cultures. Zeus-Ahuramazda, for example, wears the high Mithraic tiara of Persia, but the winged thunderbolts of Greek Zeus are carved around his diadem. So to the last detail Antiochus was concerned to keep the balance even. The tomb is a monument to the pride and sacred fervor of this King of Commagene, but it is also a celebration of the marriage of Greece and Persia, arranged by Alexander the Great three hundred years before Antiochus came to the throne.

Guardian eagle from the west terrace

The west terrace seems to have been a smaller replica of the east terrace. Here, too, the monumental gods sat in a row, gazing steadily before them. The courtyard was smaller, being closer to the edge of the mountain, and there is no trace of a fire altar. All the sculptures seem to have been carved by the same hand.

Most of our present knowledge of the tomb on Nemrud Dagh comes from the devoted explorations of the American archaeologist, Theresa Goell, who first visited the site in 1947. Unknown to the West until discovered by a road engineer, Charles Sester, in 1881, it was examined briefly by German and Turkish archaeologists in 1882–83, and was then largely forgotten. Theresa Goell organized a series of expeditions in 1953–56, 1958, and 1960, under the auspices of the American Schools of Oriental Research, in the hope of discovering the original plan of the *hierothesion* before earthquakes and erosion reduced so much of it to floating rubble.

There was a host of unsolved problems. By what roads did the priests and pilgrims reach the shrine? Were the eastern and western terraces exactly complementary? What purposes did they serve? How were they connected? What was the explanation of the long undecorated wall of the north terrace? What had happened to the head of Apollo-Mithras, missing from the east terrace? Where were the accommodations of the priests, musicians, and temple slaves? How much of the tumulus was rock, and how much a rubble surfacing? Would new inscriptions be found to supplement those already known? Since Antiochus was evidently buried beneath the tumulus, where was the entrance to the tomb?

Most of these questions have now been answered. The work remains unfinished, however, because every question raises more questions and the design becomes more intricate the more it is studied. From the beginning Theresa Goell was confronted with monumental difficulties. Nemrud Dagh lies in an isolated corner of Turkey two days journey on foot from the nearest town where supplies can be secured. Daytime temperatures reach 130° F., and the temperature on the mountain sinks to freezing point at night. There are no trees for shade, no lumber for shoring up the ruins, no wood for fuel. All must be hand-hewn in the deep valley settlements and hauled up the mountain by men and beasts. There is no protection against dust-storms, rain, and hail except the wind-tossed tents and trenches in which she and her colleagues often took shelter. Bears prowling for food and roving wolf packs often threatened the camp and the pack animals sheltering there.

Nevertheless the work went on. The terraces were cleared, and it was discovered that the colossal statues which seemed to rise at the top of a wide monumental stairway actually stood on a terrace of their own cut from the living rock. Below them, set against the rock face, were limestone reliefs showing Antiochus being received by the gods, with stairways at each end. In 1953 a passage was dug through the rubble along the bases of the statues, enabling Dr. F. K. Doerner and Kermit Goell, the brother of the director, to make rubber latex copies of the inscriptions, and here they found the missing head of Apollo-Mithras lying on the bedrock. In the following year, a tunnel was dug through the rubble immediately behind the figure of Zeus-Ahuramazda in the hope that this would lead to the tomb, but after digging seventeen feet the living rock of the mountain was encountered. They found no tomb entrance. No more boring was undertaken, as the rubble was continually slipping and endangering the workers.

The most profitable finds were made in clearing the east and west terraces. Here were found the Persian and Greek ancestors of Antiochus carved in light relief, some damaged beyond recovery, others, like the portrait of Darius I sunk in thought and wearing a Persian tiara studded with stars, in a perfect state of preservation. A two-headed lion was found, becoming a three-headed lion a year later when the third head was found. Edicts written in a beautiful and ornate Greek script were found on rocky outcroppings in the neighborhood, and these were copied by Kermit Goell by means of liquid latex which produced a mirror-image. Bit by bit the huge sanctuary on the mountain top was made to reveal its secrets. The tomb chamber, however, has not yet been discovered.

Relief of Mithradates (father of Antiochus I) and Hercules, found at Arsameia on Nymphaios, near Nemrud Dagh

We can only guess at the real appearance of Antiochus, but we know how he saw himself. Nearly always he is seen wearing the rays of Apollo in his crown, and there is the smoothness and beauty of Apollo in his features. He wears a Hellenistic mantle over his Persian vestments, the tunic looped up to reveal the tight-fitting trousers; five lions' heads decorate his sword-scabbard, there is a jeweled torque round his throat, and winged thunderbolts and processions of lions appear on his diadem. Dressed in all his panoply, he is the equal of the gods and one of them. He clasps hands with Hercules, who is naked, though a lion's skin trails behind him; and in the gaze and expression of Antiochus there is a simple friendliness, as of a man who is well-received by the gods. It is what one might expect from the man who wrote: "I, Antiochus, have raised this place to my own glory and that of my gods."

Relief of Darius I from the east terrace

Fresco of a goddess from a Roman tomb at Ashkelon

# ASHKELON

ASHKELON is among the world's most ancient cities, with the ruins of all ages lying beneath the earth. Origen says there were famous wells dating from the time of Abraham, and there were others who spoke of a city on the cliffs possessing fleets of warships and merchantmen long before the time of Abraham. It was known to Ramses II who conquered the city and celebrated its capture with a carving showing his soldiers breaking through its gates on the walls of the temple of Karnak. This happened in the ninth year of his reign, which would correspond to 1283 B.C. Nearly thirteen hundred years later Herod the Great, who was born in the city, spent a fortune adorning it with palaces, baths, fountains, and colonnades. In A.D. 65, when the rebellion against the Romans broke out in Palestine, the Jews set the whole town on fire.

Among the Roman remains in Ashkelon are the recently discovered vaulted tombs. There is nothing remotely suggesting the armed might of the Romans in these tombs, which are covered with frescoes in soft pastel shades. We see nymphs bathing and hounds hurrying through the underbrush. There are exotic traceries of leaves and tendrils. Rivers wind through meadowlands, and the face of Apollo appears through the branches of a tree. On the dome of one of the tombs a crowned goddess, Demeter or Juno, looks down protectively upon the sarcophagi. The painting is flaking away, but enough remains to suggest an artist who painted with great boldness and a deep sympathy. The goddess is both regal and gentle. Her shoulders are broad, and she could carry the dead in her arms. Trees, branches, and leaves crowd round her. The artist seems to be saying that death is no more than a lying down in the shadow of trees, and soon the sunlight will come again and the faces of the gods and goddesses will be seen through the leaves.

Cross with fish and pomegranates from a mosaic floor at Shavei Zion

# SHAVEI ZION

EARLY in 1958 some German Jews living in the small settlement called Shavei Zion (Returners to Zion) on the rocky Mediterranean coast between Acre and Lebanon decided to build a road to link their community with the outer world. They acquired a bulldozer, and they had hardly begun to work on the road when the bulldozer bit into some fragments of a pavement which showed signs of having once been scorched by fire. The archaeologist Moshe Prausnitz was summoned, for it was evident that the scorched pavement was many centuries old. Gently the pavement was lifted up. Underneath were found two layers of mosaic, both forming the floors of a Christian church.

There was nothing surprising in the discovery of fourth-century Christian mosaics along this coast, for all of Syria at that time belonged to the Byzantine Emperors. What was surprising was the discovery of a Christian settlement of which all historical traces had been lost. Moshe Prausnitz came to the conclusion that the church and the town surrounding it had been burned to the ground in A.D. 540 when the Persian Emperor Khosrau I, taking advantage of the absence of Justinian's armies in the west, swept through Syria and destroyed everything in his path. Aleppo and Antioch were sacked and burnt, and the same fate seems to have befallen this obscure town on the coast.

An astonishing number of crosses have been found in the mosaic floors of Syrian churches, all of which must have been designed before A.D. 427, when the representation of the cross was forbidden by law. The exquisite beauty of the cross at Shavei Zion arises from a curious balance between the central medallion and the flaming, rainbow-colored sunburst surrounding it. The *tesserae* are formed of vivid red, blue, and white stones, so arranged that they give an impression of innumerable colors. The fish leaping towards the pomegranates seem to have been symbolically arranged to represent the Syrian coastline.

The white marble statue from Caesarea

# CAESAREA

BUILT ten years before the birth of Christ, Caesarea has long ago tumbled into ruins. Here Pontius Pilate kept his official residence, and St. Peter converted Cornelius the Centurion, and St. Paul was imprisoned. Here, too, the Crusaders under St. Louis of France built fortresses against the Saracens, and the Genoese discovered the green crystal chalice they called the Holy Grail. Herod the Great designed it to be the chief port of Rome's eastern colonies, and for this reason named it after Caesar.

Today Caesarea, abandoned after its destruction by the Arabs in the thirteenth century, is coming to life again. The ruined harbor is being restored; the small amphitheater built by Pontius Pilate and furnished with marble seats has been completely excavated; and work has begun on the excavation of the immense Hippodrome, which is known to have been as large as the Colosseum at Rome. The chief synagogue of Byzantine Caesarea has also come to light. Little by little ancient Caesarea, with its temples and synagogues and churches, is being recovered from the earth.

Statues, too, are beginning to appear, not always where they were expected. In the spring of 1951 a tractor working in the fields a little to the east of Caesarea brought to light a great statue of red porphyry, clearly depicting a Roman Emperor. The statue was headless and armless, and could not be identified. A few days later another statue of white marble was discovered nearby. This, too, was headless and armless. The Israeli Department of Antiquities was then informed, and excavations began, resulting in the discovery of a Byzantine pavement and a triple archway. The statues had evidently flanked the archway of a building which may have been a Hadrianaeum, a temple raised in honor of the Emperor Hadrian. A strange inscription in Greek, referring to a hitherto unknown governor of Caesarea, was found nearby. It read: "Under the Governor Flavius Entolius the mayor Flavius Strategius built out of public funds the wall, the steps, and the apse in the tenth indiction. In a good hour."

No one knows for sure what the inscription means, but it would seem that a Greek mayor amused himself by looting statues and building a temple as much in his own honor as in honor of the Roman Emperor.

The white marble statue shows the Emperor, or perhaps a god, naked to the waist, one leg tucked under him, and the knees widely spaced. The folds of the *himation* are magnificently sculpted, and the whole figure suggests imperious power.

# TABGHA

He saith unto them, How many loaves have ye? go and see. And when they knew, they say, Five, and two fishes.

And he commanded them to make all sit down by companies upon the green grass.

And they sat down in ranks, by hundreds, and by fifties.

And when he had taken the five loaves and the two fishes, he looked up to heaven, and blessed, and brake the loaves, and gave them to his disciples to set before them; and the two fishes divided he among them all.

And they did all eat, and were filled.

ON the shores of Lake Galilee, on the site where the miracle of the multiplication of loaves and fishes traditionally took place, a Byzantine church was erected in the fifth century A.D. On the recently uncovered mosaic floor of the church an unknown artist represented the scene outside the church gate. He put in the water tower which still stands, the trees and oleander bushes and lotuses, and all the birds—doves, ducks, herons, cormorants, and geese—which lived near the church. Peacocks disport themselves along one border. A snake attacks a heron, winding its tail around the heron's leg, and does no harm. Two baby ducks float on a lotus, while on another lotus a baby cormorant flaps its wings. Everything about the mosaic is joyful, artless, and spontaneous. There is no design, only a gay improvisation.

The Church of the Multiplication stands just outside the village of Tabgha near the seven springs from which it derives its name, Tabgha being the Arabic equivalent of the Greek *heptapegon,* meaning seven springs.

Mosaic of a snake attacking a heron from Tabgha

Peacock mosaic from Tabgha

# BETH SHE'ARIM

TEN miles west of Nazareth, on the southern slopes of the Galilean highlands, there lies the little village of Shiekh Abreiq, indistinguishable from hundreds of other villages around. Here long ago was the town of Beth She'arim, founded by the Hasmonaeans, which was to become a great center of Jewish learning and the seat of the Sanhedrin under Rabbi Yehudah Hannassi, Patriarch of Galilee, after the Romans made Jerusalem uninhabitable by the Jews. In this town Rabbi Yehudah completed his work on the Talmud about the year A.D. 200, and about this time Beth She'arim became the main cemetery for Jews not only of the Holy Land, but also for the entire Middle East as far as Mesopotamia and even southern Arabia. Beth She'arim acquired in fact some of the sanctity which had fallen on Jerusalem.

Underneath the town a whole catacomb city was carved out of the soft limestone, and for more than two hundred years burials took place there, the last occurring about the year A.D. 415. Surprisingly often the Jews used Greek and Roman motifs, testifying to the pervasive influence of Greece and Rome on Jewish culture. The living figures of lambs and lions and other animals, hitherto forbidden, are represented. This underground world seems to have been deliberately planned to convey a sense of continuing life, and it furnishes convincing proof of a particularly strong belief in the resurrection of the dead at this time.

The first excavations were made between 1936 and 1940 by the Jewish Palestine Exploration Society under the guidance of Professor Mazar, who later became President of Hebrew University. After an interval of ten

Stone door from the necropolis at Beth She'arim

The catacombs of Beth She'arim

The "Shell Sarcophagus"

years, the excavations were resumed under Dr. Avigad of Hebrew University, who discovered new catacombs of enormous size, one of them containing two hundred huge sarcophagi, most of them with roof-shaped lids, so that a visitor has the impression of walking through a street of quiet houses. Here, too, were found representations of human figures, and this was perhaps the greatest surprise of all.

The carvings on the sarcophagi have a gentle gaiety. Two lions guard a tomb. They have sharp claws and sharp teeth, heavy manes and curling tails, but no one could take them seriously; they are more like children's playthings than roaring lions. A more richly ornamented tomb, known as the "Shell Sarcophagus," has lions and an eagle playing about on it in charming confusion. Though the tomb is massive, it is given an effect of lightness by intricate lacy designs, and the lion represented at the right under a shell-like archway is even less than a child's plaything: It resembles the little woolen dolls one gives to babies. Nevertheless, the tomb gives an impression of a majestic if casual work of art. Here a synthesis of many styles reaches perfection.

Very often the artists were concerned to make stone imitate wood. A heavy stone door is carved with patterns applicable only to wood. This door, dividing two subterranean galleries, seems to have been deliberately designed to suggest to the awakening dead that they are living in houses very like the houses they had lived in before. A seven-branched candlestick is carved on the walls. A horseman carved in soft limestone on one of the interior walls is carrying a sword, but he seems to be only waving farewell. The prevailing spirit in these catacombs is perhaps best revealed in a recently discovered Greek *graffito* on the walls. "*Eutykhōs ti humon anastasi,*" reads the happy inscription: "Good luck in your resurrection."

"Sarcophagus of the Two Lions"

Horseman with a sword at Beth She'arim

Mosaic of the chariot of the sun at Beth Alpha

# BETH ALPHA

DURING the first half of the fourth century A.D. the Jews for the first time began to decorate the floors of their synagogues with colored mosaics, usually adapting themes derived from pagan sources. For reasons which are still unknown, the strict laws against making graven images were abandoned. The rabbis no longer denounced the making of images; they merely enquired into questions of propriety, saying that some images were proper and permissible, while others were questionable, and still others were anathema. The Emperor, of course, could not be represented in any form. Under no condition could there be representations of crowns, swords, spheres, rings, serpents, or eagles, for these were the symbols of foreign domination. Soon there came a time when nearly everything that was purely decorative was permitted. The synagogues began to flower with mosaics.

The floor of the synagogue at Beth Alpha near Bethshan to the south of the Sea of Galilee is almost completely covered with brilliant and intricate mosaics dating from the early sixth century A.D., brought to light by workmen digging an irrigation ditch in 1928. We see Abraham about to sacrifice Isaac, while the hand of God descends from the heavens and the ram waits in the thicket with a legend reading: "Behold, the ram!" We see the Torah Shrine and the *ner tamid*, the Eternal Light, guarded by lions, and there are representations of most of the objects used in the Jewish liturgy. The most completely successful mosaic takes the form of a central panel showing the chariot of the sun surrounded by a zodiac circle, with angels representing the four seasons at the corners. This central medallion is clearly a copy of a Greek or Roman work, but the artist has deliberately given a peculiarly Jewish weight and power to the design. The youth guiding the chariot is recognizably Apollo, but he is a Jewish Apollo. The horses are recognizably horses, but no Greek or Roman artist would have depicted them in this way. The sun-god wears a six-fold crown, stars are scattered over his legs, and his body is formed of rainbows. His brilliant gown is entangled in the wheels of his chariot, but he drives forward with an extraordinary air of authority and severity. The horses, however, have no severity. They seem to be laughing with sheer joy over some secret joke of their own.

# HAZOR

THE once powerful city of Hazor lay in the Jordan Valley between Lake Huleh and the Sea of Galilee. For five hundred years, from about 1700 B.C. to 1200 B.C., it was the center of a small empire ruling over all of Canaan. The city stood on a mound overlooking an easily defended plain to the north, and was rich and populous; it has been calculated that 40,000 people lived there during the time of its greatness. Sometimes the armies of the Pharaohs swept up to the city gates, and from time to time

Temple relics from Hazor in the Haifa museum

a royal edict would announce its capture; but the Pharaohs announced its capture too often to be completely convincing. When the Kings of Astaroth and Tyre complained to Pharaoh, the King of Hazor contented himself with a contemptuous reply. About 1200 B.C. Jabin, King of Hazor, in alliance with neighboring tribes fought against Joshua at the waters of Merom, and his army was defeated. The Book of Joshua goes on to describe the fate of Hazor:

> And Joshua at that time turned back, and took Hazor, and smote the king thereof with the sword: for Hazor beforetime was the head of all those kingdoms.
>
> And they smote all the souls that were therein with the edge of the sword, utterly destroying them: there was not any left to breathe: and he burnt Hazor with fire.

So Hazor fell, and with it died the civilization of the Canaanites. It was not perhaps a very great civilization; but objects uncovered from the ruins by an army of determined excavators under the direction of Dr. Yigael Yadin, the famous soldier-archaeologist, under the auspices of the Hebrew University of Jerusalem, testify to an extraordinary calm and composure. The lion in the bas-relief found in the Canaanite temple at Hazor gives an impression of complete relaxation. He will stir himself, if forced to; he will watch and guard, but he will not attack for the sake of attacking. It is the same with the ritual figures. They sit calmly on their thrones and gaze straight before them, undisturbed and unafraid. Near

Relief of a lion from Hazor

the sanctuary of the temple there was found a storeroom containing a potter's workshop, with the potter's wheel still lying where it was abandoned when the city fell. Lying nearby was a ritual mask which had just been completed. This mask with its large eyes and arched brows, rather prominent ears and sensitive mouth, hints at the character of these people. Holes on the forehead, and below and above the ears, show how the mask was worn.

**Ritual mask from Hazor**

For two or three centuries after its destruction by Joshua, Hazor remained uninhabited. Then gradually the city flickered into life again. Under Solomon it was rebuilt and fortified, becoming a garrison city for his chariot troops, and in the time of Ahab and his successors it had regained most of its former power and importance. In 730 B.C. the

Assyrians razed it to the ground for the second time, but even then it did not die completely. Through Assyrian, Persian, Hellenistic, and Maccabean times the citadel continued to be defended. Then finally, no longer possessing any strategic value, it was abandoned.

Hazor presents fantastic problems to the archaeologists. The city spread out over the immense northern plain, and most of this must be excavated if the entire history of Hazor is to be revealed. On the citadel itself there are layers upon layers of fortifications, layers upon layers of temples. There are the fortresses of King Jabin, of Solomon, of Ahab, of Pekah, of the Persians, and of the last Hellenistic conquerors. Though he has been provided with a large army of helpers, Dr. Yadin has recently announced that it would take 800 years at the present pace to complete his excavations.

# CYRENE

ON a high plateau near the sea in modern Cyrenaica lie the crowded ruins of the ancient city of Cyrene. According to the legend, Apollo wooed the nymph Cyrene "of the lovely arms" and made her his bride after seeing her kill a lion singlehanded. She became the patroness of the city when it was founded by Greek settlers from the island of Thera about 631 B.C.

Ruins at Cyrene

Cyrene developed rapidly, and soon its kings became powerful figures in North Africa. "You are a king over great cities, and this great privilege is a shining heritage of your house," wrote the poet Pindar in an ode addressed to King Arcesilaos IV of Cyrene in 462 B.C. Another king, called Magas, was sufficiently famous to be mentioned in a monument set up by King Asoka in India. He ruled for fifty years, led his armies against Egypt, and died at last, "suffocated by his own bulk." Till the time of the Roman conquest Cyrene remained a power to be reckoned with, deriving its wealth largely from the export of a strange plant, *silphium*, believed to have medicinal qualities, and now extinct.

Destroyed during a Jewish revolt in A.D. 115, and again during a great earthquake in A.D. 365, Cyrene always rose from its ashes. It survived the decline of Byzantine power in Africa, and the march of the Arabs to the Atlantic. Then gradually it fell into decay. By A.D. 800 its history was over. Then there were only the tumbled ruins, the streets and theaters and temples, on the rocky plateau looking out towards the Mediterranean.

In 1860 two English archaeologists came to Cyrene and carried on extensive excavations on behalf of the British Museum. They discovered a colossal statue of Apollo playing on his lyre, and some 150 cult statues. All of these were sent to the British Museum, and it was generally believed that everything of importance had been carried away. Little was heard of Cyrene until 1913. In that year the Italians took possession of Cyrenaica, and in the winter a torrential rainstorm brought to light the beautiful Venus of Cyrene, which is the principal prize of the Museo delle Terme in Rome. Two years later the Italians found a colossal nude statue of Zeus lying face downward. For twenty-six years, from 1913 to 1939, the Italians continued their excavations, completely uncovering the sanctuary of Apollo and a large part of the forum area. Since World War II the excavations have been continued by the Cyrenaican Department of Antiquities.

The little-known museum at Cyrene is filled with Greek sculptures from all periods. Archaic *korai* stand beside sculptures which must have come from Periclean Athens, and others from Hellenistic times. The superb, deep-chested Hermes was found in the Roman baths, but he is a Greek original of the fourth century B.C. This powerful athlete wears the head of a young philosopher. Mind and energy are balanced in a sculpture of formidable attainment. One feels he could tear a mountain to pieces with his bare hands or divert rivers with a single sweeping gesture; and he would know the causes of mountains and rivers.

The Hermes from the Roman baths at Cyrene

Hellenistic Aphrodite from Cyrene

The Venus is a companion piece to the Venus of Cyrene, perhaps by the same artist. By leaving her head intact and chopping off her fingers, fate has made it nearly impossible for the observer to concentrate on the young and nubile body: we are only too aware of a senseless mutilation. Headless and armless, she would perhaps be more beautiful. The head of a young Hellenistic prince has been sliced off at the crown, and his entire body has perished. It seems hardly to matter. All that we want to know about him is vividly made known to us in that eager and sensual face.

In the northern necropolis of Cyrene were found a number of strange monuments, with short columns surmounted with stone wigs instead of heads. The folds of the women's gowns are elaborately and delicately carved by a sculptor with a feeling for the flow of archaic draperies. Row upon row of these faceless figures decorated the necropolis, and no sculptures that would fit over the columns have been found. Were painted wooden mortuary masks attached to the columns? Did sculptors carve features into the columns? No one knows.

The three-headed goddess Hecate, queen of the night and messenger of the underworld, has rarely been represented convincingly, for a three-headed goddess almost defies a sculptor's powers. Yet this fourth-century Hecate found in the sanctuary of Apollo is only too convincing. Beautiful and imperious, with cavernous eyes, she gazes watchfully at the three corners of the world, and we are made aware of the terror in her gaze. Power streams from her, as it streams from so many of the figures found in Cyrene, far from the Greek mainland. Here in North Africa the Greek sculptors left some of their greatest treasures.

Hellenistic male portrait

Faceless tomb figure from the necropolis at Cyrene

The goddess Hecate from Cyrene

The "Time Mosaic" from Haidra

# HAIDRA

IN the winter of 1939 some workmen at Haidra in Tunisia came upon a mosaic of the third century A.D. entirely unlike any Roman mosaic found up to that time. The characteristic heaviness of the Roman mosaicist was absent. Here everything was lightness and grace, swift flowing lines, a deliberate exclusion of exact symmetry. North African and perhaps Egyptian feeling are combined with Roman precision to make a mosaic which has the appearance of a rich carpet.

A surprisingly large number of ancient mosaics are concerned with time, here represented as a naked youth enclosed within the ring of the zodiac. The youth is clearly an African, probably of Berber stock. He stands with flashing eyes within time's circle, one arm wrapped round the zodiac, the other waving a sheaf of wheat, while the seasons revolve around him at his command. The sheaf of wheat is perhaps a magic wand.

The four seasons are represented at the corners as winged cupids, each attended by a brace of birds and by seasonal plants. Spring, shown at the left-hand corner, wears a skimpy leopard skin as he wanders through a garden of roses with a peacock and peahen on either side. Summer, at lower right, wears a sun helmet and carries a sheaf of wheat almost as large as himself. Pheasants accompany him as he wanders through the wheat fields. Summer is bronze and sturdy; but Autumn is pale again, and there is something appropriately awkward in his expression as he plucks the grapes and places them in a wicker basket. He is attended by herons.

Winter shivers among olive trees. No longer naked, he wears boots and a heavy woolen cape with the hood thrown over his head; in one hand he carries a brace of ducks; in the other a birdlime snare. Two geese accompany him on his journey. He looks older and wiser than the other cupids, and indeed he scarcely resembles a cupid at all.

Though the four seasons are placed in the four corners of the mosaic, the artist has so arranged the twelve ovals that the square mosaic is given a sweeping circular movement, suggesting the revolutions of the heavens. There is no stillness, no place where the eye can rest after it has left the figure in the central medallion. Vines, roses, wheat ears and olive branches race towards the center and turn back again in continual flux. Time is seen as energy, as fecundity. The artist has created the intricate tracery of leaves and flowering branches with an extraordinary sureness of hand. The heavy meander pattern of the border has the effect of giving a three-dimensional feeling to the whole mosaic. The mosaic probably decorated the floor of a bath. It is quite small, being scarcely more than ten feet square.

In the spring of 1961 the mosaic was presented by President Habib Bourguiba of Tunisia to the United Nations in New York, where it is now set in one of the walls.

# INDEX